Teaching Practical Ethics for the Social Professions

Edited by Sarah Banks and Kirsten Nøhr

© **European Social Ethics Project (ESEP) 2003**

All rights reserved. No reproduction, copy or transmission of this publication may be made for profit-making purposes. Copying parts of book is allowed to use for teaching. Some of the material in the book and additional material can be found at http://www.durham.ac.uk/community.youth/ESEP/ESEP.htm

Price of book: 19 Euros
Distribution of book: Please see websites of ESEP or FESET

ISBN 87-989486-0-1

Cover design: Susanne Whitta Jørgensen
Cover photo: Pelle Rink
Layout: Grafisk Himmel, Copenhagen, Denmark
Print: Narayana Press, Odder, Denmark

Published by:
FESET
Formation d'Educateur Sociaux Européens
European Social Educator Training
www.feset.dk

Contents

Acknowledgements

We are grateful to FESET for contributing towards the funding of this book, and for continuing support for the work of the European Social Ethics Project. We are also extremely grateful to the schools, colleges and Universities that have both contributed towards funding the publication and supported the participation of the contributors. The contributing institutions are listed below.

We would like to acknowledge the support of the University of Durham, in particular a grant through the Research in Learning and Teaching Scheme, which has enabled Angela Emerson to work on developing the ESEP website and Sarah Banks to devote time to this project during 2002. We are also grateful to CVU København & Nordsjælland for supporting Kirsten Nøhr in overseeing the production of the book.

Members of the European Social Ethics Project and supporting institutions

Sarah Banks, University of Durham, UK
Isabel Baptista, Universidade Portucalense, Porto, Portugal
Adalberto Carvalho, Universidade Portucalense, Porto, Portugal
Wilfred Diekmann, Hogeschool van Amsterdam, The Netherlands
François Gillet, Haute Ecole de Bruxelles, Belgium
Henk Goovaerts, Katholieke Hogeschool Limburg, Belgium
Helene Jacobson Pettersson, University of Kalmar, Sweden
Robert Langen, FHS Hochschule für Technik, Wirtschaft und Soziale Arbeit St. Gallen, Switzerland
Anne Liebing, Roskilde Pædagogseminarium, Denmark

Maarit Miettinen, Humanities Polytechnic, Tornio Unit,
  Finland
Birgitte Møller, Københavns Socialpædagogiske Seminarium,
  Denmark
Nils-Erik Nyboe, Danner Seminariet, Denmark
Kirsten Nøhr, CVU København & Nordsjælland, Denmark
Frank Philippart, Hogeschool Brabant, Breda, The Netherlands
Maria Pidello, Fondazione C. Feyles, Torino, Italy
Françoise Ranson, I.R.F.F.E., Amiens, France
Dalija Snieskiene, Vytauto Didžiojo Universitetas, Kaunas,
  Lithuania
Karin Stenberg, Malmö Högskola, Sweden
Aira Vanhala, Oulu Polytechnic, Finland
Jochen Windheuser, Katholische Fachhochschule
  Norddeutschland, Osnabrück, Germany

The ESEP group can be contacted through:
http://www.durham.ac.uk/community.youth/ESEP/ESEP.htm

Former members of the European Social Ethics Project

Marieke Linnebank, Hogeschool van Amsterdam, The
  Netherlands
Michael Nieweg, Hogeschool van Amsterdam, The Netherlands
Katariina Ylipahkala, Humanities Polytechnic, Tornio Unit,
  Finland
Anna Zielinska, Akademia Pedagogiczna, Krakow, Poland

1.
Introduction

Sarah Banks and Kirsten Nøhr

The European Social Ethics Project

This book has been compiled by members of the European Social Ethics Project (ESEP). The project began at a FESET seminar in Brussels in Autumn 1998 and has involved teachers from over 20 training institutions in a variety of different European countries. The current and past membership of the group is listed at the beginning of the book. The aims of the project are to develop our understanding about:

- how students conceptualise and talk about ethical dilemmas and problems;
- what kinds of issues they find problematic;
- how education and training can better prepare them for the ethical dimensions of practice.

We have been particularly interested, as teachers, in exploring how we can encourage students to develop the qualities, skills and understanding to work out how to act in difficult situations involving ethical dilemmas and problems. The concept of the 'reflective practitioner' (Schön, 1987, 1991) has been influential in our thinking about professional education, as has the 'project method' of studying, which has been adopted particularly in Denmark and Holland (see articles by group members: Nieweg, 2001; Nøhr, 2001).

Members of the group have undertaken several small research projects using individual questionnaires and video-recordings of group discussions that have been designed to enable us to learn more about how students learn, as well as developing teaching and learning materials (for more details see Banks, 2001 a; Banks & Williams, 1999). Some of our ideas were put into practice and new ones developed in Spring 2002 in an intensive teaching and learning programme with students and teachers from several different European countries funded through the European Commission's Socrates programme.

The aims of this book

This book draws together some of the materials and the learning developed through the work of the group over the last four years. Its aim is to present a selection of ideas on teaching practical ethics for teachers involved in the professional education of students in the fields of social work, social care work, social pedagogy, social education, youth work and community work. It does not aim to be a comprehensive workbook, nor does it aim to cover ethical theory in any detail. Rather, it is a compilation of approaches, tools and techniques that we have found useful in our teaching, in the hope that it may be of use to others also.

The social professions

We are using the term 'social professions' to encompass a range of related but often distinct occupations that are variously configured in different European countries as: social work; social care work; social pedagogy; social education; youth and community work. In each country, the terms used for these occupations and the types of roles they play varies. But broadly speaking, these occupations comprise practitioners whose role it is to work with people who are regarded as in need of support, advocacy, informal education or control. They work within a shared set of values stressing a commitment to individual and social change, respect for diversity and difference and a practice that is participatory and empowering. In the chapters that follow, we use the term 'social professions' to refer to this range of occupational groups. When referring to particular contexts, the contributors may speak of 'social care workers' or 'youth and community workers', for example, but quite often we have used 'social worker' as a generic term for practitioners working in any of the social professions. 'Social worker' in this sense is used more broadly than its more common usage to refer simply to one of the social professions.

What are/is ethics?

Before proceeding further it is also important to state how we are using the term 'ethics'. This is not an easy question to answer, particularly as the term is used in several different ways in English, with variations in other European languages. 'Ethics' (in the plural) can be used to refer to the norms and standards of behaviour people follow concerning what is good or bad, right or wrong. But it can also refer to the study of these norms and standards (a singular term). These two uses of the term can be further broken down, as shown in Box 1.1. Regarding the first usage of 'ethics', in English we often use the terms 'ethics' and 'morals' interchangeably. Indeed, 'morals' is derived from the Latin ('mores') and 'ethics' from the Greek ('ethos'), both of which mean habits or customs. It is in this interchangeable sense that we will use the terms 'ethics' and 'morals' in this book, along with the adjectives 'ethical' and 'moral'. However, it is important to point out that some commentators do distinguish between the two terms (see, for example, Bouquet, 1999).

Box 1.1: Meanings of 'ethics'

1. **The norms and standards of behaviour people follow concerning what is good or bad, right or wrong**. In this sense ethics may mean either:
   a) *particular norms and standards* (for example, 'the ethics of truthtelling') or
   b) *a system of norms and standards* (for example, 'Buddhist ethics').

2. **The study of the norms and standards of behaviour people follow concerning what is good or bad, right or wrong**.
   In this sense ethics may be divided into:
   a) *meta-ethics* – the study and analysis of the meanings of moral concepts such as 'good' or 'right' and the nature of morality (regarded as part of the discipline of moral philosophy);
   b) *normative ethics* – giving answers to moral questions about what course of action is right or wrong – for example, whether abortion is always wrong (often regarded as part of moral philosophy or religion);
   c) *descriptive ethics* – what people's moral opinions and beliefs actually are – for example, whether the majority of people in Europe believe abortion is always morally wrong (often regarded as part of sociology or anthropology).

This is a very general description of how we use the term 'ethics'. It does not tell us what gives an ethical dimension to a particular situation, motive, action or decision. How do we recognise a situation as involving an ethical issue or an ethical problem or as having ethical implications?

Any event or situation has practical, technical, political and ethical dimensions. But these are not inherent in the nature of the event itself, they are constructed by the actors involved in the situation, or commentators reflecting on it. Pulling out the 'ethical' dimension is inevitably artificial, as it is deeply embedded and intertwined with the practical, technical and political elements. The following example may help to indicate what we think gives a situation an ethical dimension:

> A volunteer is putting up a shelf in a community centre. Last week she promised the youth group that it would be fixed before their next session, which is today in 30 minutes time. The volunteer only has two sizes of screws: small and large. Neither is the right size for fixing the shelf. She may see her choice as merely a technical dilemma – choosing between the small screws that might not support the shelf, and the big screws that would be extremely difficult, perhaps impossible, to fit. But this situation could also be construed as having ethical dimensions. The manager of the centre may come along and ask how safe the shelf will be, expressing concerns about the risks of it falling and hurting someone and suggesting the installation is delayed until the right screws are obtained. The choice may then be seen as not just between two technically imperfect solutions, but between risking human safety versus breaking a promise. Adding the dimensions of 'human safety' and promise-keeping brings the situation into the sphere of the 'ethical'.

The subject matter of ethics is the welfare of living beings. This is a broad area to cover; most situations and events have a dimension relating to the welfare of humans or animals if we look hard enough. But we tend to focus more on the ethical dimension when there is a difficult choice to be made – when a problem or dilemma occurs. An important issue for us in working with students is developing their capacities to perceive a situation as having an ethical dimension.

Practical ethics in professional life

Although many of the members of the European Social Ethics Project do use ethical theories developed by moral philosophers in their teaching, the work of this group has focused very much on how students experience ethical issues in practice, rather than how we apply ethical theories to professional life. We have deliberately used the term 'practical ethics' as we wish to stress our concern with what Callahan (1998, p. 58) describes as: 'the kind of ethical inquiry that takes as its direct concern the resolution of concrete morally problematic cases and issues of moral urgency in the lived world'.

We use the term 'ethics' (as the study of norms of behaviour) in a very broad sense. We are not just concerned with the application of general ethical principles or the use of reasoned argument to make decisions or justify professional actions (a 'principle-based' approach to ethics). We are also interested in the role played by emotions, in how the particular details of the complex situations in which professional practitioners find themselves are taken account of, and how moral qualities such as care, compassion and attentiveness play a role (a 'relationship and character-based' approach to ethics).

For there has been a tendency in professional ethics in recent years to focus on the articulation of general moral principles of action and their use in making decisions and justifying actions by means of deductive rational argument, moving from general principles and derived rules and applying them to particular cases. This has been the dominant focus of much Western thinking on ethics since the Enlightenment, typified by the theories of the eighteenth-century German philosopher Immanuel Kant (1964) based on the ultimate principle of respect for individual persons and their rights, but also represented in the Utilitarian principles of promoting welfare and justice (Mill, 1972). A recent critique of this approach has advocated a revival of 'virtue ethics', as expounded by Aristotle, Aquinas, and more recently MacIntyre (1985), where the focus is on the goodness and badness of the motives and character of the people making ethical decisions, as opposed to the rightness or wrongness of the actions they take. This is related to, but distinct from, what has been termed an 'ethic of care' that has often been put forward by feminists, who suggest that in making ethical decisions it is important to consider the nature of our relationships to particular other people (as opposed to general principles about how all people should be treated) – our commitments, roles and responsibilities (see, for example, Noddings, 1984; Sevenhuijsen, 1996; Sevenhuijsen, 1998; Tronto, 1993). There may also be a role for emotion in ethics, for empathy and moral sensitivity, which the rational, principle-based approach ignores. This is particularly stressed by those who emphasise the importance in ethics of the face-to-face encounter with the other person (Levinas, 1984, 1989; Løgstrup, 1997). Box 1.2 distinguishes between these two broad approaches to ethics: principle-based approaches and character and relationship-based approaches (see Appendix 1.1 for a short summary of each approach, and Banks, 2001b for a more detailed discussion).

Box 1.2: Some approaches to professional ethics

I. Principle-based ethics

a) **'Kantian' principles**, for example:
- respect for persons;
- self-determination of service users;
- respect for confidentiality……..

b) **Utilitarian principles**, for example:
- promotion of welfare/goods;
- just distribution of welfare/goods.

II. Character- and relationship-based ethics

a) **Virtue ethics** – development of character/virtues/ excellences, such as:
- honesty;
- compassion;
- integrity ….

b) **Ethic of care** – importance of particular relationships, involving:
- care;
- attentiveness;
- responsibility…..

We do not believe these (and other) theoretical approaches to ethics are mutually exclusive. In professional life, the use of general principles, impartially applied and justified with reference to reasoned arguments, is very important. In the social professions we work with many clients or service users, and it is important that we treat them fairly, without favouritism or personal preference. On the other hand, we are often working with people who are very vulnerable, who have specific problems, and who enter into relationships of trust with us. It is therefore important that we take account of the unique circumstances of each person's life, that we express care and compassion, that we exhibit empathy and act in ways that honour the trust placed in us by the people with whom we work. One of the most important moral qualities of a professional practitioner is that of empathy and the ability to perceive a situation as one of moral significance. As James Rest (1994, p. 22) comments:

> There is widespread agreement that there are more components to morality than just moral judgement. The trick, however, is to identify more precisely what else there is in morality, and how all these pieces fit together.

Rest (pp. 22-26) identified four components of moral behaviour, which can be summarised as follows:

1. *Moral sensitivity* – awareness of how our actions affect others. This should also include what Vetlesen (1994) calls 'moral perception', which involves the use of the faculty of empathy (a disposition to develop concern for others) to see the morally relevant features of a situation ('the features that carry importance for the weal and woe of human beings involved');
2. *Moral reasoning or judgment* – the ability to make critical judgements regarding moral values and various courses of action;
3. *Moral motivation* – placing moral values above competing non-moral values;
4. *Moral character* – having certain personality traits, such as courage, perseverance, and high self-esteem, that predispose us to act morally.

All these components are important when considering how students develop into ethically sensitive and reflective practitioners. Whilst moral reasoning or judgment is very important, the other components are equally valuable, although we often do not regard them as being part of the domain of ethics.

Tools for teaching professional ethics

The chapters in the rest of this book offer some ideas about methods and materials that can be used in teaching practical ethics for the social professions.

Chapters 2 to 8 discuss various approaches to engaging students in discussion, analysis and reflection through the use of methods such as: case-based discussion; video-recordings; reflective diaries; Socratic dialogue; problem-solving and decision-making models; and drama. These chapters outline approaches that could be used with students, giving guidance for teachers on how to facilitate groups using the different methods. Some of the chapters are illustrated with examples from the authors' own teaching experiences, or from some of the work done with students in the European Social Ethics Project.

The next two chapters give accounts of how a whole curriculum or event on ethics can be developed. Chapter 9 discusses the development of the ethics curriculum at one particular University, while Chapter 10 focuses on the organisation of a European Intensive Programme on ethics for students and staff from nine institutions. These two chapters bring together some of the approaches and techniques discussed earlier and show how they can be put into practice creatively. The account given in Chapter 10 of the intensive programme on ethics involving staff and students from many countries demonstrates an impressive depth and quality of student learning. Finally, in Chapter 11, an annotated selection of literature recommended by members of the European Social Ethics Project as useful for teaching ethics is presented. References for all the chapters are gathered at the end of the book.

The ESEP is also developing a website for use alongside the book at: http://www.durham.ac.uk/community.youth/ESEP/ESEP.htm. It will contain some of the materials mentioned here, which can then be downloaded for use directly in class. At present the materials are in English, but over time we will collect materials in different languages, and invite our readers to contribute cases or methods they find useful in their work.

Appendix 1.1:
A brief overview of some theories of ethics

1. Principle-based ethics

a) **'Kantian' ethics** – named after the eighteenth-century German philosopher, Immanuel Kant (1724-1804). In professional ethics certain aspects of 'Kantian' ethics are stressed – particularly the ultimate principle of 'respect for persons'. He formulated this as a categorical imperative (a command that must be obeyed), one form of which is: 'So act as to treat humanity, whether in your own person or that of any other, never solely as a means but always also as an end'. By this he meant that we should treat others as beings that have ends (that is choices and desires), not just as objects or a means to our own ends. The individual person is intrinsically worthy of respect simply because she or he is a person, regardless of whether we like the person, whether she or he is useful to us or has behaved badly towards us. According to Kantian philosophy, a 'person' is a being who is capable of rational thought and self-determined action, where 'rational' means the ability to give reasons for actions; and 'self-determining' entails acting according to one's own choices and desires and having the ability to make decisions. 'Respect' can be regarded as an 'active sympathy' towards another human being. The principle of respect for autonomy (freedom of choice) of individual persons is, therefore, very important within Kantian philosophy. This is echoed in the principle of self-determination in social welfare ethics.

Lying, deceiving, stealing from or manipulating another person are regarded as always morally wrong for Kant. For Kant, the moral worth of an action lies in the nature of the action itself, regardless of its consequences (for example, even if lying would produce a good result, it is still morally wrong and I should never lie). For Kant, a right action is one done from the motive of duty. He was also very concerned with consistency and 'universalisability' in moral judgements. So, for example, it would not be morally right for me to lie to get myself out of difficulty on a particular occasion, because we could not logically argue that it should be universally accepted that lying to get oneself out of difficulty is morally right.

b) 'Utilitarian' ethics – is particularly associated with two British philosophers, Jeremy Bentham (1748-1832) and John Stuart Mill (1806-1873). In contrast to Kantian ethics, the moral worth (rightness or wrongness) of an action is said to lie in its consequences. Many versions of utilitarianism have been developed, but the basic idea of utilitarianism is very simple: that the right action is that which produces the greatest balance of good over evil (the principle of utility). So, for example, if lying would produce a good consequence, then lying would be right. But it is recognised that the question of 'whose good?' is an important one, which is where the principle of justice comes in, that the good should be as widely distributed as possible. That is, the right action is that which produces the greatest good of the greatest number of people. Philosophers have disagreed over what counts as good: whether is just pleasure or happiness, or it includes truth, virtue, knowledge, and so on. The principles of promoting welfare and justice in social welfare ethics can be seen to relate to utilitarian ethics.

II. Character- and relationship-based ethics

a) Virtue ethics – is associated with the ancient Greek philosopher, Aristotle (384-322), although there are many other versions, including a recent revival of interest in virtue ethics. What they have in common is a focus on the character or dispositions of moral agents as opposed to abstract obligations, duties or principles for action. One of the reasons suggested for the growing popularity of virtue ethics is a view that principles are too abstract to provide helpful guidance in the complicated situations met in everyday ethics. According to virtue ethics an action is right if it is what a virtuous person would do in the circumstances; a virtue is a character trait a human being needs to flourish or live well. What counts as 'living well' or 'flourishing' then becomes an important question in deciding what characteristics count as virtues. Some virtue theorists argue these vary according to different time periods and cultures (for example, the kinds of characteristics cultivated as virtues in ancient Greece may not all be applicable in twentieth-century Europe); others claim that there are universal virtues. Nevertheless, the kinds of dispositions usually regarded as virtues include courage, integrity, honesty, truthfulness, loyalty, wisdom and kindness, for example. A virtuous person will tell the truth, it would be argued, not because of some abstract principle stating 'you shall not lie', or because on this occasion telling the truth will produce a good result, but because that person does not want to be the sort of person who tells lies. Virtue ethics also tends to emphasise the particular relationships people have with each other. It could be argued that it makes more sense to see my kindness towards my best friend as arising out of the fact that I have a relationship of friendship with her, I like her and care about her, rather than from some abstract moral principle about promoting the welfare of others. There is debate about the extent to which such an approach can be applied to professional life, such as in the social welfare field, where some universal principles or rules seem necessary to guard against favouritism, for example.

c) The 'ethic of care' – this type of approach to ethics has been associated particularly, although not exclusively, with modern feminist philosophers. While having some similarities in approach to virtue ethics, it has been argued that virtue ethicists have tended to focus on virtues such as justice, courage, honesty and generosity, while paying little attention to the kinds of virtues needed in order to help others. Recent developments of an ethic of care owe much to the empirical work of psychologist Carol Gilligan who identified two 'moral voices' in her interviews with people about how they conceptualised and spoke about moral dilemmas (her book, *In a Different Voice*, was published in 1982). She contrasts the 'ethic of care' with what she calls the 'ethic of justice'. The ethic of justice refers to principle-based approaches to ethics, including Kantian and utilitarian moralities, which are based on a system of individualised rights and duties, emphasising abstract moral principles, impartiality and rationality. Gilligan argues that this is a very male-oriented system of morality, which does not take account of approaches to ethics that tend to be adopted by women. This would emphasise responsibility rather than duty and relationships rather than principles – an 'ethic of care'. Gilligan herself is equivocal about the extent to which an ethic of care should be regarded as a 'female' or 'feminine' ethics, although others in this tradition explicitly adopt this kind of view. Some attempts have been made to develop an ethic of care for nursing.

2.
Writing and using cases

Sarah Banks and Nils-Erik Nyboe

Introduction

This chapter explores what we mean by a 'case' in the context of teaching ethics for the social professions, and offers some guidance about how to write and use ethics cases in teaching.

What is a case?

In the social professions we often talk about a 'case' when we mean a person, a family or a group with whom we are working. A 'case' can also be a short description of a situation, an event or a piece of work. This is what we mean by a 'case' here. Sometimes we use the term 'case study', which indicates that the case may be used for learning and teaching. We may also speak about a 'vignette', or even a 'story'. We are using the term 'case' here to cover all these variations.

In professional education it is quite common to make use of cases in teaching. They give an account of a real or fictional situation, describing the important features. They may describe everyday events and actions that students will encounter in their practice, or, more commonly, they may be used to describe situations that are constructed as problematic – involving a difficult decision, a dilemma, or a situation where 'mistakes' have been made.

Whether we are writing a case about a real situation or a fictional one, the case is always 'constructed'. That is, we decide what features of the situation are relevant for our purposes. So, how we write the case will depend on how we want to use it. And how the case is written will to some extent determine how the students respond to it. So it is important to think carefully about how we want to use a case before we write it. Cases can be long or short; detailed or schematic; contextualised in time and place or relatively abstract.

Use of cases in teaching

Cases can be used in a variety of ways. The following list gives some examples:

1. Students can be asked to analyse cases (perhaps identifying what are the main issues involved) individually or in groups;
2. Students can be asked to analyse cases individually or in groups and then come to a decision about what should be done/should have been done in this situation;
3. Students can be asked to undertake further research into the issues raised by a case (this can be used as part of 'project work' with students working together in groups);
4. A case can be used by the teacher, or by the author of a textbook, to demonstrate how a situation that commonly arises in practice, or a difficult situation, can be analysed, understood or resolved – for example, a textbook may include a case where a practitioner has to decide whether to break confidentiality, and then a commentary is written on the case by the author, or an expert in the field (see, for example, Banks, 2001b, pp. 160-185; Levy, 1993).

We are mainly concerned in this chapter with the first two uses of cases.

The typical 'ethics case'

Chambers (1997, p. 172), in discussing cases in bioethics, claims that 'ethics cases' are distinctively different from professional cases in general. Of course, sometimes we may use a general case, and ask students to pull out the ethical issues. But quite often, if we are teaching professional ethics, we tend to construct an 'ethics case'. Our students will also have expectations about what to look for in the case if they think it is connected with ethics.

Below we give an example of an ethics case we have used in the European Social Ethics Project. It has been modified from an account written by a British social work student who was asked to write an ethics case. The teacher then condensed the case and rewrote it for use in teaching.

Case example 1: Under-age sex and helping the police – A 12 year-old girl, Kerry, was admitted into a residential home on a voluntary basis as her parents were unable to cope with her 'out of control' behaviour. Kerry looked older than 12 (she could have been taken for 15) and had been disowned by her parents because of her sexual activity. She had been having sexual relations with Mr A., aged 40-50 years, since the age of nine. He had picked her up in a playground. In exchange for sexual favours, he supplied Kerry with money and cigarettes. According to the student working in the residential home, Kerry valued these gifts, but not herself. At one stage the police were close to arresting Mr. A., but needed some more evidence. The police asked the staff of the home to remove the restrictions on Kerry leaving the home, in order that she might go and meet Mr. A. and then police could catch him 'in the act'. The student asked the question, should we refuse because in helping the police we would be allowing Kerry to put herself at risk, or is catching Mr A. and preventing further risk a priority? What should the staff do?

Chambers distinguishes four features of an ethics case: reportability; action; tempo; and closure. We will apply these features to the case above.

1. ***Reportability*** – like all good stories, there is a 'plot'. Something happens. Quite often in an ethics case this involves an ethical transgression or an ethical dilemma or problem. In this case there are many morally relevant features: for example, under-age sex is taking place and the police have asked the staff of the home to make what is perceived as a difficult and potentially risky decision.

2. ***Action*** – ethics cases tend to be stories that are driven by their 'plot'. They have a focus on action – what is done, what happens, rather than on the setting in which it happens or the characters of the people involved. So, for example, few words are usually used to describe the place where the action happens. In fact, the action could take place in any country, at any time. People's character traits are rarely represented – usually only when they relate to the cause of actions. We do not know whether this case is set in England or Denmark or anywhere else. We do not know if the setting is a private home, a large home, and so on. We know little

of Kerry's character, apart from her 'out of control' behaviour and the fact that she looks older than she is. Nothing is said of the 'staff' of the home, or the student involved. They have no names.

3. **Tempo** – usually ethics cases are short – that is, they take a short time to read. But often they may summarise what happened over a long period of time ('summary'), and they miss out many events over that time ('ellipsis'). The tempo of the story often relates to the entrance of the main characters into the world of the social professions (we do not hear about what happens when they are outside this setting). In the case above, what happened with Kerry and Mr A. between the time when she was nine and 12 is summarised in a few lines. Other aspects of Kerry's life in addition to her relationship with Mr A. are not covered.

4. **Closure** – very often an ethics case may end with a question: 'what should the practitioner do?' or 'What would you do if you were the person involved?'. They ask the reader to bring closure to the story. The case may either lack an ending, or ask the reader to rewrite the story. Chambers (1997, p. 181) refers to the structure of tragedies, which may be extended to cover all stories. Stories begin with an exposition (a description of the situation), followed by a complication (a problem, dilemma or complexity), then a reversal, and finally a resolution to the conflict. Quite often in an ethics case, no resolution is given, or if it is, the reader may be expected to rewrite the ending according to how they think the participant(s) *should* have acted. If the reader thinks the ending given is satisfactory, and it does not need rewriting, then it would not be regarded as an ethics case. An ethics case requires a high degree of participation by the reader. In the case above, the situation is not given an ending. Indeed, a question is framed at the end in the words of the student as a choice between two alternatives. Many ethics cases are more open-ended than this one, simply ending with asking the reader to say what should be done.

The limitations of typical ethics cases

Chambers comments that the construction of ethics cases in this way tends to encourage their analysis in terms of principle-based approaches to ethics (as outlined in the Introduction to this book). That is, we would tend to analyse what is happening in the case and what should be done in terms of impersonal and impartial principles and rules, because we are not given any details of the context in which the action takes place, the character or motives of the people involved, their past histories and relationships, their hopes and fears. So in the case of Kerry above, we may frame the issues, as the student does at the end, in terms of a choice of action where, perhaps, the rights of Kerry to be respected as a person (and not to be used or deceived in order to catch Mr A.) are weighed against the principle of protecting Kerry from future harm and promoting the welfare of other young people who may also be harmed by Mr A. in the future.

These points are very valid. If we think that in understanding the issues involved in a case and coming to a decision it is important to consider the details of the particular people involved and the relationships they have with each other (people who advocate an 'ethics of care' would argue this) and the motives of the people involved (virtue ethicists might advocate this), then how useful are cases like the one above?

We would argue that such cases are useful for getting students to think through the ethical issues involved in difficult situations. If we give more details of people's lives, characters and motives, then the case begins to become very long. It also becomes more complex, with too much information for students to work with. Further, the more information given, the more students ask for. The story can never be the full story.

It is also interesting that even if students are given a short case like case example 1 to discuss, they nevertheless start to construct the context themselves. This is part of the exercise of developing their moral awareness. They will ask questions and give hypothetical answers. For example, it might be asked: 'What if Kerry really feels trapped by Mr A., but is frightened of challenging him?'; 'Do the staff in the home know the police and can they trust them?' The students themselves start to bring in issues of feelings, emotions and relationships as they think they are relevant.

Even a short case, if desired, can be written slightly differently to include some mention of feelings or to create more of a sense of an atmosphere. The next case is a constructed case, given by a Dutch colleague, translated and rewritten slightly for use in the European Social Ethics Project.

> *Case example 2: A lonely child* – Hans is a 10 year-old boy living in a child protection home located in a small village. He lives in a 'group' with seven other children. It is almost Christmas and all the other children have been allowed to go home to celebrate with family and friends. Hans cannot go home because he is not welcome there. His father has just run away and his mother does not care about him. It is Christmas evening and Wilhelm is the social care worker on duty in the home. Wilhelm and the child are alone in the institution, sitting together next to the Christmas tree. The Christmas tree is already losing its needles – the counsellors in the home jokingly called it an 'acid rain tree'. Wilhelm is thinking about the situation. Even with the music on, it is very silent. Even candy, cake and drinks do not help create a festive atmosphere. Clearly this burden is heavy for Hans. Wilhelm thinks of his own Christmas tree at home: his pride and joy, green and full. What should Wilhelm do?

This case has several references to feelings, emotions and atmosphere. It makes reference to Hans's mother not caring about him. Wilhelm is said to be 'thinking' about the situation, and about his own home. There is mention of a 'burden' that is 'heavy'. The 'atmosphere' in the home is mentioned. The fact that is it Christmas, which many readers (depending on their cultural origins) will associate with family and festivities contrasts with the 'heavy' atmosphere depicted in the home. From these small 'hints', students can then pick up and develop further thoughts and questions about this case which might refer to: the relationship of Wilhelm to his own family and the other boys in the home; how Hans might feel if offered some other alternatives; what does Hans really want; is it the worker's role to lift the burden or to stay with it? These and many more issues and questions have been raised by the many students who have discussed this example in groups, or written down their responses individually, in addition to the obvious, but unstated question raised by the case: 'Would it be right for Wilhelm to take Hans home' or, put more broadly, 'is it right to mix one's personal and professional lives' (see Banks & Williams, 1999 for a discussion of students' responses to this case).

So, in our opinion, it is not necessary to write long and detailed cases with lots of references to feelings, motives and relationships in order to get students to discuss these aspects of a case. Of course, the questions the teacher asks students to consider in relation to a case will also influence how they respond. Another way of encouraging students to get in touch with the feelings of the characters involved in a case is to ask them to do a role play based on the case (discussed later in this chapter).

Using short cases with students individually

One of the ways the ESEP has used cases like those given above has been in the form of a questionnaire for students to answer individually. We did this as part of a small exploratory research project (to see how students responded to ethics cases) and it has been used with students as a preparation for a European intensive programme, as discussed in Chapter 10. We have also used it in the course of our everyday teaching. It can be a good way of starting a class, to be followed by a group discussion.

In Appendix 2.1 we give an example of a questionnaire we have used with students, asking them to write down their responses to cases individually first, and then to work in small groups sharing their responses. After the sharing in small groups, they were then asked to note down individually whether and how their views had changed as a result of the group discussion. This encourages students to reflect on their own values, presuppositions and perspectives. Many students report that they change their views, or that their ideas broaden in talking through the issues with other students (see Chapter 10). Asking them first to write down their own views enables them to track their own changes in opinion, or the way in which their views may have been confirmed or clarified during the discussion. Although students often resist working on their own at first, and may express a desire to discuss with others prior to writing down their own views, it is useful for them to have done some thinking on their own before coming to the group discussion. It gives them the opportunity to think through some possible ideas and arguments, so they are prepared for the work with the other students.

Using short cases in group discussions

Cases such as those shown above, or several more given in Appendix 2.2, can be used simply as a starting point for a group discussion. Students can be asked to work in small groups (usually about six, but groups of any size between two and eight can be successful) discussing the case, noting their findings, and then reporting back in turn to the larger group led by the teacher. The differences and similarities between groups can be noted – particularly any new perspectives or noticing of particular features of the situation. If the course has involved input on ethical theories, then students can be asked to relate their answers to relevant ethical theories. But this is not essential.

Examples of the kinds of questions students could be asked to discuss might include:

1. *What are the ethical issues involved?* This is to encourage students to identify the morally relevant features of the situation. For example, in case example 2 above, students might mention issues such as caring for the individual, fairness of treatment, the duties of the professional worker, the promotion of welfare, protection from harm, and so on.

2. *How did these issues arise?* This is designed to encourage students to clarify their understanding of the case further, and to think about what factors might have influenced or brought about the situation. For example, in case example 2, you might expect students to mention the fact that Christmas is a special time in many cultures; nobody seems to have anticipated the 'lonely' situation and made plans to make it better; and so on.

3. *What action would you take and what ethical arguments would you use to justify this?* This is designed to encourage students to discuss possible courses of action and be able to say why they would act in a certain way. You might expect them to refer to ethical theories, principles or rules, where appropriate, or simply give reasons to back up why they would choose a particular course of action. For example, a student who decided simply to stay in the care home over Christmas with Hans might give arguments about the importance of keeping personal and professional life separate, or about not wanting to treat Hans as a special case, as this might be regarded as unfair by the other boys, or cause Hans to expect more in the future, and so on.

Alternatively, if students have been explicitly taught about ethical theories, they could be asked the following question:

> Identify the ethical issues in this case, then consider what you would do if you were the practitioner involved, using: i) a Kantian approach; ii) a Utilitarian approach; iii) a virtue ethics approach. Do these theories help?

Longer, more detailed cases

There may be occasions when a longer and more in-depth case is appropriate. If, for example, students are to be asked to work on a particular case over several weeks, to research the issues involved and possible solutions (as might be the case if they were using a case as part of a group project, or in a problem-based learning context), then more details of the characters involved and the context would be helpful. It may then be less appropriate to invite closure, or at least students may be invited to investigate a range of possible resolutions (as outlined by Windheuser in Chapter 7). Alternatively, the point of the exercise may not be to find an ending or solution at all, but rather to explore the issues.

Students can be asked to write up cases themselves from their own experience, which can then be used in class discussion. In Chapter 4, Banks suggests that students may write up cases raising ethical issues during their periods of fieldwork practice as part of the process of keeping a placement journal or learning diary. Instructions can be given to students along the following lines:

> **Preparing a case**: Think of a situation/event that raised/is raising ethical issues for you in your practice. Give a brief account of this in about a page. There are no hard and fast rules about how to write this up, but it may be helpful to think of it as a narrative of an ethical dilemma and as a problem to be solved. The narrative tells a little story in four or five compelling paragraphs and includes all of the morally relevant actors and events, as well as significant times and places. It is a good idea to change the names of key people involved, to protect their identity.

The case below was written by a Dutch student and translated for the ESEP project. It tells her story of what happened on a day's outing in relation to a particular woman. The woman is of Indonesian origin. Indonesia was formerly a Dutch colony and at the time of independence in the late 1940s, many Indonesians came to Holland. This case includes references to the student's feelings, and it tells us what she did. If students are asked in class to look at this case, they might be asked to analyse and discuss the issues raised, but not necessarily to rewrite the ending (although some might choose to say what they would have done if they were the student involved).

> **Case example 3: A day's outing** – For my fieldwork practice I am working at a nursing home for psycho-geriatric patients. The group consists of 11 women and one man, all of Indonesian birth. My tasks range from organizing activities to daily care of the residents. One of the residents is Ms L., an Indonesian woman of 75 years old. She has only lived for a short time in the home. There are moments when she's completely confused, but there are also moments when she is very capable of saying what she wants and what she thinks. I find her a very impressive woman: quite small and tender, but with an iron will. When her mind is clear you cannot fool her in any way. She compels respectful treatment.
>
> One day we were going to visit the zoo in a nearby town. It was an hour by bus from the home. Two staff members would accompany the group: my supervisor and me. It is common to ask, before departure, if anyone needs to visit the bathroom – at least to ask those residents

who can tell whether or not they need to go. I asked Ms L. if she needed to go to the toilet before we got on the bus. Since it was early in the morning, most residents were quite clear. Ms L. was no exception and she answered she really did not need to go. I explained to her that the trip would take an hour, during which time she could not visit the bathroom. She said: 'Well, alright then' and I helped her out of her chair and to the bathroom. Indeed, she did not need to pass even a little water so I knew then that she was able to feel if she needed to go or not.

My supervisor had seen me leaving with Ms L. to go to the bathroom. Just when I was helping Ms. L. with her panties, she entered and gave me an incontinence pad, asking if I would put it on Ms L. I was a bit surprised and asked: 'But why, she isn't incontinent, is she?' My supervisor said that indeed she wasn't, but since it was going to be such a long journey it was best to be on the safe side. So I said to Ms L., who was just dressed again, that we had forgotten to do something. It was obvious that she did not understand why and therefore asked me why this was necessary. I gave her the same explanation that my supervisor gave to me.

Ms L. said it was absolutely not necessary and she would certainly say when she needed to go to the bathroom. The incontinence pad was enormous, while Ms L. was small and slim. She added: 'Oh no! It's such a terrible thing, much too large and much too warm!' So I tried once more, this time with a smaller sized pad, but Ms. L. kept refusing. Now it was clear enough for me: in spite of all the arguments she still was not going to wear the pad. Since I was definitely not going to force the thing into her panties, I said: 'All right, guess what: if you really don't want it then promise me to say it to me whenever you need to go, wherever we are'. 'But of course!' she said. I knew she suffered from dementia, but at this moment I felt that it was more important that she should keep her dignity than that I was following the rules. I would rather take the risk of making a mistake and be responsible for the consequences, than have it all my way.

When we left the bathroom my supervisor was standing in the hallway. She asked me if I succeeded. I explained to her why I did not put the pad on Ms. L. Then my supervisor took the pad from my hands and said to Ms. L.: 'Please come with me' and pushed her back into the bathroom. She closed the door and there I stood. I felt quite stupid and was far from happy with what was going on. In my opinion it was completely against the will of the client. Nevertheless I had to set aside my frustration since there was a lot to be done. Later my supervisor told me Ms L. was wearing the pad.

Later that day, when we had a little time, I told my supervisor that I was unhappy about what happened and I asked her why she did this. She said that she expected me to be surprised but it was necessary with Ms. L. She could be quite hard-headed and sometimes two people were needed to convince her to do or accept something. I still had my second thoughts: it was probably more for our own comfort than that of Ms. L. But I decided not to discuss the matter any further because my supervisor could feel that I was giving her a hard time. It was best not to be too critical and to keep the peace between us.

Students could be asked to discuss this case in groups. Or they could be asked individually to give a brief reflective analysis of the situation. An example of how this case might be analysed is given below:

1) Identify the ethical dilemmas or problems from your point of view – for example in the case above, one of the dilemmas for the student may have been the conflict between respecting Ms L.'s request and doing what the supervisor asked. The student also had a problem in deciding to what extent she should challenge her supervisor afterwards – she may have felt it was important to state her views about taking some risks and treating residents as adults capable of making their own informed choices, yet she was aware that she needed to keep on friendly terms with her supervisor, who would, after all, be assessing her.

2) Consider how and why these issues arose:
a) Factors specific to this case – there may have been bad experiences in the past of residents being incontinent during journeys; the student is inexperienced and does not have the attitude of 'it is better to be safe than sorry' that the other staff may have; the staff might have many other things to attend to, in looking after the residents at the zoo, and toileting needs might have complicated an already difficult outing; the student is in a relatively powerless role.
b) General factors – older people are not given as much respect as they might be in our society, nor are people with mental health problems; there is a tendency to treat people classified as 'psycho-geriatric' as incapable of making their own decisions; in residential care it can be easy to slip into a 'parentalist' regime, especially if there are shortages of staff; people from minority ethnic groups (Indonesian in this case) are often treated less respectfully and experience negative discrimination.

3) What reasons would you give for the action you took? What does this tell you about your own values? Do these values differ from those of others involved? The student in the case overleaf justified her action of not putting the pad on Ms L. in terms of respecting Ms L.'s dignity. She put this above 'following the rules'. This suggests that for her a key principle/value in her work is respecting the dignity of the individual people she works with. She was prepared to risk making a mistake and take the consequences. The supervisor either had a different view of the likelihood of Ms L. needing to go to the toilet (she assessed the risk to be quite high and was not prepared to take it), or had a different view of dignity (for example, dignity is about not sitting in a bus with wet pants) or placed less value on the choice and dignity of residents (respecting individual rights) and more on the overall comfort and efficiency of the whole outing for staff and residents (looking for the outcome that would produce the greatest good of the greatest number of people).

4) What else could you have done, or what else could be done in the future to address this or similar situations? Could the student have pursued the matter further with her supervisor, raised it at a staff meeting, questioned 'the rules'? Do the rules or practices of the residential home need reviewing or changing? Should the supervisor have made a point of working through the issues with the student and explaining the utility of her approach?

Using cases as a basis for role play

Cases written by the teacher, or brought in by students (whether described verbally or in writing) can be used as the subject of a role play in class. This can help students explore how a situation may be experienced from the perspective of a particular character, and may give the opportunity to rehearse how alternative responses to a situation could be acted out. For example, in the case above, three students could be asked to take on the roles of the student, supervisor and Ms L. A short scenario based on the student's written account could be acted out. Feedback could then be taken from the 'actors' in the role play, and comments made by other students observing the action. The observers could be asked to look out for words, actions and movements that they think might signify respect, lack of respect or parentalism, for example. Suggestions might be made for alternative types of response that could be made by the student to the supervisor, and the person playing the student could act these out. One of the observers might then take over the role of the student to try out a different response, which could then be evaluated by the 'actors' involved and the observers. Care should be taken to 'debrief' the actors (asking how it felt for them in the role) and teachers need to be aware of emotions that can be stirred up by role play and be prepared to handle these. Some of these techniques are explored further by Langen in Chapter 8, and the work of Augusto Boal, the Brazilian theatre director is also useful when considering how we reach and work with people's emotions (Boal, 1992, 1995).

The advantages and disadvantages of using prepared cases

Cases prepared in advance by the teacher, or taken from a textbook, can be written, or rewritten, to ensure that they raise the issues the teacher wishes to cover. If teachers are a little unsure about using ethics cases, then they can analyse the cases themselves in advance, and be prepared to raise questions or issues students may not raise themselves.

However, students sometimes complain that the cases are too artificial – they do not seem real. This can be counteracted by basing the pre-prepared cases on real situations. Material from previous students, practitioners, newspaper reports or television documentaries can also be written up as short cases (for example, a case of child abuse involving social workers).

Asking students to submit their own cases in advance, or asking them to describe a problematic case on the day of the class obviously makes the issues more real, and the student involved can be asked for further information. A mixture of real and hypothetical cases, of cases prepared in advance and drawn from the class on the day, will make for a varied and interesting learning experience.

Conclusions

Cases are a useful way of stimulating ethical reflection. They ground discussion in 'real life' and can be used to illustrate the application of different ethical theories and approaches and to develop students' skills in ethical awareness, ethical argument and ethical decision-making. Their usage is very versatile, as some of the later chapters in this book also illustrate. Cases can be used in the context of individual students undertaking the work of analysis; discussion and decision-making in groups; or role play exploring actions and emotions.

Acknowledgements

We are grateful to students in Britain and Holland, professional colleagues and members of the ESEP for contributing the cases. In particular, we would like to thank the student from Hogeschool van Amsterdam who wrote the case 'A day's outing' and Michael Nieweg for translating it.

Appendix 2.1:
Using cases in questionnaires for students to complete individually

Example of a questionnaire

(Note: the spaces between questions have been reduced in this version. A spaced questionnaire ready for use in class can be downloaded from the website).

Part 1 asks you to answer questions about two cases. They are very brief, and you may feel you would want to know a lot more about each case before you could decide what to do. But try to work with just the facts you have here. You may not have experience yourself in the kind of work described in the cases (for example, as a residential social care worker or as a youth worker). However, imagine yourself as an outsider looking at the situation and think about what the ethical issues are, and how you think the worker should act, given what you know about the situation. *Fill in the left column of the questionnaire on your own, without talking to anyone else.* Later, you may discuss the cases with your fellow students in groups and record any changes to your initial views in the right column.

Part 2 asks you to make some comments about your views of the values of social education work. *First answer question 2.1 on your own.* Then make some comments (questions 2.2-2.5) after you have had a group discussion with other students on the values.

Part 1 – Please read the cases and then answer the questions in relation to each case

Case 1 – A young woman, Connie, aged 24, lives in an institution for people with learning disabilities (mentally disabled people). Connie is generally quite reserved and shy, but she has had some short, very violent and self-destructive fits. On one occasion she cut herself in the abdomen with a pair of scissors. After this event the staff tried to teach her to masturbate. Her self-destructive fits disappeared when she got into a sexual relationship with a young man at the institution. About six months ago she began a relationship with a 43 year-old man (also with learning disabilities) whom she met at the local day centre. At this time she was taking the contraceptive pill, but she has now stopped. This man is well-known to the staff as he has had relationships with several female residents and has infected two of them, as well as Connie, with venereal disease. Connie has just met the man again and has told the staff that they are engaged to be married. The staff have tried several times to discuss the issue of possible pregnancy, the advantage of using contraception and eventually getting sterilised, but Connie is not interested in their opinion. Last time they discussed it, Connie told the worker in a provocative voice that she thought it would be cool to have a little doll-baby. She has just announced that her boyfriend is coming to see her on Saturday and that he is going to stay overnight. What should the staff do?

Case 2 – A youth worker is employed to work in a youth centre in an inner city area. He has been doing some street work with a group of about 20 young people aged 14-20 years who congregate on street corners near the centre. They have a passion for Indie and rave music, and over half of the group admit to using drugs (mainly Ecstasy and LSD). The group complained of boredom, so a contract was drawn up with them, enabling them to use a room in the centre twice a week to play their music. They agreed that no illegal substances would be brought into the centre and that they would not come in under the influence of drugs. With the odd exception this agreement was kept, and the worker began working with a sub-group on issues around drugs. Problems emerged when a drug dealer known to some of the young people started hanging around outside the centre. Due to his close contacts with the young people, the worker had information that would be likely to lead to the arrest of the dealer. Colleagues and the majority of the members of the centre's management committee urged the worker to go to the police. The worker knew that this would mean losing contact with the young people and being labelled as a 'grass' (an informer to the police). He felt he had been making some progress with them on harm reduction strategies. What should he do?

Individual Comments	*Comments after discussion*
1.1. What is your initial reaction to this case, including any feelings you may have about it?	
1.2. In your opinion, what are the ethical issues involved in this case?	
1.3. Would this case present a dilemma for you if you were the worker involved? YES ___ NO ___ *(Please tick)* Please explain why:	
1.4. What further information would you need before deciding what to do in this case?	
1.5. On the basis of the information you have here, how would you act in this case if you were the worker?	
1.6. What reasons would you give for deciding to act in this way?	
1.7. What kinds of new ethical problems might arise as a result of your decision?	
1.8. Do you have any further comments you want to make?	

***Part 2 – Reflecting on your answers to the questions about
Cases 1 and 2***, think about what this tells you about the values/ethical
principles you think are important for you as a social pedagogue/social
educator/specialised educator/social care worker/community and youth
worker (choose the correct title for your own country). Then answer the
questions.

2.1. What do you think are the most important values or ethical principles you hold as a social educator/social care worker/community
and youth worker?

2.2. After discussing the important values in a group with other
students, are there other important values you would like to add
to your list? If so, what are they?

2.3. How useful was the group discussion of cases and values?
(please tick one of the following):

Very useful ___   Quite useful ___   Not very useful ___

Any comments about why:

2.4. What did you learn from the group discussion?

2.5. Please let us have your views about a) how easy and b) useful you
have found completing this questionnaire and having discussions
with other students. *(Please tick)*

a) Very easy___ Quite easy___   Difficult ___ Very difficult ___
b) Very useful ___Quite useful ___ Not very useful ___

Any further comments?

Appendix 2.2:
Some more short case examples

Note: we have given these cases titles to help identify what they are about. When using them with students, it may be preferable to give them numbers (such as 'case 1', 'case 2', and so on) to avoid a prejudging of the ethical issues involved.

Cultural conflict – The worker in an Asian women's project was approached by a member whose daughter, Asha, attended the young women's group. The mother was concerned about her daughter's behaviour as she had been seen in the community with her white boyfriend. This had provoked great censure within the community as she was seen to be too 'westernised and moving out of her culture'. As a widowed single parent, the mother was quite distressed about her daughter's behaviour and the implications this would have for her own honour and respect, as well as that of her other daughters, within the community. She asked the worker to use her influence to dissuade the young woman from seeing her white boyfriend. Asha had also discussed the issue with the worker and clearly stated that she felt she should have the right to make her own decision about her future partner and did not really care what her community thought of her. What should the worker do?

Theft – A young man, well known to the local youth worker who had been supporting him in his efforts to seek work, came into a youth centre trying to sell some hi-fi equipment. The worker asked where it had come from and was told that it belonged to his father who was replacing his system. His two friends confirmed his story, and another young person agreed to buy the equipment from him. The next week, other young people, concerned for the young person buying the equipment, informed the worker that the equipment had been stolen. They clearly expected the worker to tell the police and the buyer. The worker agreed to consider the situation carefully. What should the worker do?

Residential care and violence – A 12 year old boy, Jimmy, was admitted into a residential home on a voluntary basis as his father was unable to cope with his hyperactive and aggressive behaviour. Jimmy is a very uncertain youngster, who has lived in a violent environment all his life. He seeks a lot of attention and tries to be careful about how he treats other people. However, Jimmy does not have enough skills and patience to establish positive and lasting relationships with other young people and educators. Jimmy becomes the 'scapegoat' of the group and an increasing number of incidents are happening. Jan, the tutor-educator for Jimmy pleads with the team to treat Jimmy more leniently, to use 'positive discrimination' towards him, to give him time to find his place in the group. During a conflict, Jimmy reacts violently and it seems certain that he will be sent away from the institution. What should Jan do?

3.

Using video in group discussions

François Gillet, Sarah Banks, Kirsten Nøhr
and Françoise Ranson

Introduction

This chapter explores the making and use in teaching of video-recordings of students discussing ethical issues. Suggestions are given as to how a small group of students can be video-recorded, and how subsequent viewings and transcriptions of tapes can provide useful material for analysis. Work with videos offers an opportunity to enhance students' and teachers' understandings of how ethical interpretations and arguments develop in relation not just to the verbal content, but also non-verbal behaviours and group interactions.

Why use video?

When students discuss ethical issues we often tend to focus on words and arguments only. What is said? How are reflections brought about? What do the students think and how do they argue for their opinions? How is new recognition developed? All these questions are important when we discuss and make decisions about how to act when confronted with ethical problems and dilemmas. Using video recordings of the discussions, however, adds new dimensions to the analysis and gives both teachers and students the possibility to keep the taped discussion and go deeper into the analysis. Making and retaining a video gives students the opportunity to observe and reflect on issues in a way that they are unable to do if they are participants (or even observers) of real-time social events. The video allows us to view and review what people say and do, compare differing interpretations with one another and reduce our reliance on recollection in favour of repeated inspection. Recording the discussions on video also allows us to look at the non-verbal as well as the verbal communication. Looking at images can be a good transmission of the feelings and emotions connected to the words when the debate is about ethical issues. The group dynamics also become more obvious and analysable.

How to make the video-recording

Video-recording can be arranged with a group of students discussing a case. One or more of the short cases given in Chapter 2 could be used. This way of organising the discussion gives the students a common story that they keep in mind while you ask them to debate issues arising from this particular case. The discussion could be organised in other ways, for example, around a broader ethical question.

Organising the class discussion
If you are working with a class of students, the video-recording session could be organised as a 'goldfish bowl discussion', with a small group discussing an issue and the rest of the group observing. Ask for six volunteers willing to be video-recorded discussing a case for about 30 minutes. The rest of the class should sit around the edge of the room as an audience. They should be asked not to make any comments or noise during the recording.

The six students that are being video-recorded should be sitting on chairs arranged in a semi-circle, preferably with no tables in front of them. The teacher (or other leader of the group) sits at one side and should draw his or her chair away a little after giving the instructions and should not participate in the debate. The session should be no longer than 30 minutes and can be arranged by the teacher/facilitator as follows:

1. *Preparation*: Prepare seven seats in a semi-circle. Position the camera(s) appropriately. Give out the case you are using to all the students (including the audience) and ask them to read the case silently (four to five minutes).

2. *Introduction*: Ask the six students to sit in the semi-circle. Position yourself in the semi-circle, but at one end (not in the middle). The video-recording should begin at this point. Then read the text out loud for everybody, answering any immediate questions from the group of six.

3. *First round of individual responses*: Introduce the first round, asking each student in turn to answer the question: 'What would you do if you were the worker involved?' This should be just an initial reaction and should not take more than a couple of minutes per student.

4. *Group discussion*: After each student has spoken, then invite the students to engage in a debate about the case. Withdraw slightly yourself, so that it is clear that the students are expected to discuss with each other, not with you. Allow the debate to continue for as long as you think appropriate (it may come to a natural end, or you may choose to bring it to an end after about 15-20 minutes). During the discussion you should not intervene, unless there is a very strong reason (for example, the students have got completely stuck, or one is very upset ....)

5. *Second round of individual responses*: Draw the discussion to a close and introduce the second round. This involves asking each student in turn to comment on the following: 'After hearing all those reactions, what would your first concrete decision be now?'

6. *End the discussion*: After the round is finished, thank the students and end the discussion. Stop the video-recording.

Use of recording equipment

When using video it is important to make the technical side work as well as possible. The quality of the sound and the pictures need to be good enough for the analysis that follows. There can be several ways of setting up cameras and using one or more microphones. The ideal equipment would be one panoramic fixed camera and one or two mobile ones, along with two or three microphones with a multi-track recording and mixing-system. But less advanced equipment can be used with satisfactory results. One mobile camera and a good operator will be sufficient. Adapting a directional microphone on the camera is very useful to get a good recording of each student's voice. You may also connect an external microphone located in the middle of the group. To get even more detail on the sound, you can add a simple tape recorder with a good microphone, placed in the middle of the group. This can also be useful for transcribing the debate.

While the teacher is reading the case to the group, the camera could film each of the participating students successively. This gives a good chance to observe how they react to the case. Throughout the session it is important to get a good balance in order to get reactions from each of the students.

The video-recording can be used in a number of ways with the students. It can be played back and used immediately in the teaching session with the class of students. Alternatively, or in addition, the sound recordings can be transcribed and the video-recording analysed over a period of time by a class of students, or by a small group as part of a project.

Discussing the video-recording in class

Immediately after the recording is made, the teacher might ask the six students to say how they found the experience of discussing the case and being video-recorded. This allows them to relax from the pressure of the camera and reflect a little on what went on. The audience could then be asked to comment on what they saw and heard. The video-recording could then be re-played, with students asked to observe carefully aspects of the group interactions, the dialogue and arguments used, or body language, for example.

Roles in groups
If you are using the exercise to learn about groupwork and communication you might focus on interactions between the students. For example, students could be asked to focus on one participant in the discussion and note:

- every time the person you are observing speaks;
- to whom they speak;
- after whom they speak;
- who follows them;
- how much notice was taken;
- what kind of role did the participant take.

Comparing notes from the observers can enable us to see a pattern of the dynamics in the group. And it may give us more insight in the process of taking decisions.

The use of argument
If you are using the session to discuss how moral opinions and arguments are shaped, you may focus more on the content of what is said:

- What kinds of arguments do the participants use (for example, do they focus on: individual rights; the consequences of actions; the qualities of workers)?
- How much focus is there on professional duties?
- How do they use personal experience?
- How do lines of argument develop?

Non-verbal behaviour
It is much more difficult to focus on the non-verbal expressions (see Birdwhistell, 1973, for a classic text on body-motion communication), but students could be asked to look for:

- Body movements;
- Facial expressions;
- Silent communications;
- Tone of voice.

It may be possible to try and link these to the verbal lines of argument and group dynamics. This can be quite difficult to achieve, but is part of the 'added value' of working with a video recording, as opposed to simply using audio-recordings or engaging in group discussions.

An idea that may be useful in this context is Goffman's (1971) notion of 'body gloss' which refers to the way in which individuals position and move the body (or parts of the body) to signify their alignment to what is happening in the setting. Typical things here might be: the person that comes late into a meeting or leaves a meeting early and provides a body gloss on an apology; the person who raises their eyebrows to provide a body gloss on astonishment at what someone has just said or done; the person who holds their head in their hands while someone else speaks and thus provides a body gloss on desperation, and so on.

Analysing the recording

If a group of students wishes to analyse the recording in some depth, then it will be helpful to transcribe the sound recording. In this case, it is advisable to have taped the voices separately and to have a tape recorder with an automatic rewind. This will ease the work a great deal. Doing a transcription of the whole discussion is rather time-consuming, but can also be very rewarding if you want to go into the lines of argumentation and the students' influences on each other. There are specialist methods for doing this in the field of conversation analysis (see Hall et al., 1997; Ten Have, 1999; Taylor and White, 2000), but unless the aim is to develop these kinds of skills with students, it would be advisable to aim for a rough transcription initially. If certain passages are selected for deeper analysis, then it can be useful to write down all the spoken words as accurately as possible, noting significant non-verbal expressions, breaks in the discussion, and so on (see Goodwin 1981 for some guidance about how to do this with video-recordings).

One way of working is to select one or more short verbal sequences that are regarded as important moments and connect them with non-verbal sequences: expression of voices, eyes, faces, hands and arms; attitudes of bodies and a general impression of the group dynamics. By selecting particularly strong sequences articulating verbal and non-verbal expressions, students can then work on them with video tools like slow motion, stop-on-image, cutting sound or image. It may be possible to follow how one student 'thinks about life' through his or her talking and acting. It is interesting also to see how various themes proposed by different students can influence the debate by the way the students listen – or do not listen – to each other. Even the themes that are not mentioned in the discussion can be of great importance. In the end you may be able to see what factors may have influenced the answers the students give about their future thinking and action.

Video-recording a group discussion can be a teacher's project to deepen understanding of group dynamics and development of thinking among the students. The video can be analysed by the teacher alone or together with students. The video method could also be arranged as students' own project where they work on the entire process of filming, transcribing and analysing the discussion, with the teacher as a supervisor. The goal could be, for example: to explore manifestations of ethical awareness and sensitivity: to analyse ethical thinking and its development; to explore manifestations and understandings of 'professionalism'; to explore group dynamics. Relevant questions to ask the students to analyse and answer would then be:

- Define the theme to be explored;
- Identify the questions relevant to this theme;
- Look at the video and analyse it (in small groups);
- Share the conclusions;
- Consider what you learnt.

Such a project is very time-consuming and intensive, but it is particularly suitable for students working together in small study groups, where it can also serve as a team-building exercise. In such a project, attention to the last question – to evaluate what has been learnt from the process itself – is very important.

Exploration of group dynamics: an example

Two third year community and youth work students from the University of Durham made a video-recording of a group of six second year students discussing the case of 'cultural conflict' about an Asian woman and her daughter who both turn to a worker for help (see Appendix to Chapter 2 for details of this case). The audio-recording was transcribed, and the students then worked with a tutor to select a significant extract from the video-recording to analyse. They chose a short clip where a lot of non-verbal interaction was taking place between some members of the group whilst another member was talking. This extract was then worked on further, with an attempt being made to add some basic details of the non-verbal behaviour on the written transcript. This is not easy, and requires a close watching and re-watching of the video. The transcript below is a preliminary version, adapting some of the conventions developed by Goodwin (1981, pp. vii-viii):

1. The numbers on the left hand side of the page are the line numbers given to the transcript, starting from the beginning of the tape;
2. A dash (-) marks a cut-off, and several dashes (- - -) indicate pauses;
3. A square bracket ([ ) connecting the talk of different speakers shows that overlapping talk begins at that point;
4. A capital X shows the place where eye contact is made;
5. *Italics* indicate bodily movements/gestures;
6. Round brackets ( ) indicate some speech is indistinct or missing.

100	**C:**	[The thing is, at the end of the day, the	*A's hand on*
101		community, the Asian community, is in support of	*chin*
102		the mother. The daughter, eventually if she ignores	
103		all the advice that her mother and the community	
104		are giving her, is going to be cast out and she's the	
105		one that's gonna need the support ( )	

[

106	**A:**	But, yeah, but you're saying the	*A's hand*
107		Asian com-munity is, is, possibly gonna -- support	*towards C. A*
108		the mother, and I, I, would agree actually.	*nodding.*
			C looks A

109	**C:**	They won't support the mother.

[

110	**A:**	But if, if the daughter --

[[

111	**B:**	But [

[

	B:	X ____	*B looks at A,*
			then down

112	**A:**	is sort of --- has a white boyfriend, is on ( )

[

113	**C:**	She would be
114		cast out.

115	**A:**	Yes she'll be cast out. I mean, I actually have expe-	*Arm open;*
116	[	rience of being cast out --- but --- erm --- but then	*hand on chin;*
	[		*laugh; foot up*

117	**C:**	[( ) the role of the worker ( ) young person	

[

	B:	X ____	*B looks to A,*
			then mouths
			something to
			C.

118	**A:**	the daughter will go for the --- she will, might be	

[

	A:	.... X ____	*to B*

[

	B:	... X ____	*fixed grin*
			at A

119	**A:**	cast out of that, but she will enter something else --	*D starts to*
120		I'm, I'm not saying it's straightforward.	*swallow*
121		I really am not.	

122	**D:**	I agree with A's first point that she was making
123		about about the dialogue -- side of it.

This extract comes fairly early in the discussion, when the students have been trying to establish whether the mother or daughter approached the worker for help first. They have been interrupting and talking over each other quite a lot. At line 115, A. agrees with C. that if the daughter has a white boyfriend, then the daughter will be 'cast out' of the Asian community. A. adds that she actually has experience of being cast out herself and at this point puts her hand on her chin, gives a little laugh and raises her foot. At line 116, C. speaks over A. as A. talks about her own experience of 'being cast out'. At the same time B. looks at A., then turns to C. and silently mouths something to her. A carries on talking, but is aware of the silent communication between B. and C. A. looks at B., who gives her a fixed grin (an artificial smile). D., who has said very little so far, starts to swallow as A. is talking at line 119 and then states his agreement with a comment made earlier by A.

Students A. and C. seem to be competing to offer an account of the issues at stake in the situation described in the case. A. verbally offers agreement with C. in line 108, also nodding her head, but C. immediately contradicts A. in line 109. At line 115, A. again indicates agreement: 'yes, she'll be cast out'. But C. talks over her at line 116, while B. allies herself with C. by silently mouthing something to her. When B. then responds to A.'s glance at her by giving A. a fixed grin, this is a momentary gesture, hardly noticeable. But when frozen in a frame of the video it conveys a clear gesture of ridicule and dismissal from B. to A. In his last comment, D., who has been silent for a long time, appears to be aligning himself with A., who is being challenged verbally by C. and non-verbally by B. This short extract can be analysed to show how different people's accounts and arguments compete for space and credibility on the basis not just of words, but gestures and looks too. The notion of 'body gloss' mentioned earlier can be employed to explore expressions like the 'fixed grin', or the 'hand on chin', for example.

Conclusions

There are several advantages and disadvantages of the approach suggested in this chapter. Making video-recordings is a time-consuming project and it is important to be realistic about this. Furthermore, not all students find it easy to engage in discussions while being video-taped, and some may be inhibited by the camera. So we should be careful not to over-interpret what we observe in the video – remembering that it is a constructed session, shot in a specific moment, and not giving a full picture of the students' ethical awareness.

However, using video-recordings of group discussions can enable a detailed study of how ethical arguments are expressed and developed in a group or team situation. Ethical decisions are often taken in teams, or in debate and discussion with several people. Studying video-recordings can raise students' awareness of the range of relevant explorations and arguments that they can drawn on in ethical debates, and how group interactions, both verbal and non-verbal, all influence the discussion and any final decisions. This approach is a way of integrating the study of ethics with communication. Video-recording and audio-taping also enables us to look at and listen to the discussion again and again and can develop students' skills of observation and analysis.

Acknowledgements

We are very grateful to the Haute Ecole de Bruxelles for hosting meetings of students and staff to work on the video project and providing technical assistance. We would like to thank all the students and staff from the ESEP institutions and several others who participated in the making and analyzing of videos, particularly Donna Miskin and Claire Ovington, former students of the University of Durham. Robin Williams, University of Durham, also offered some helpful comments on the analysis of videos.

4.

The use of learning journals to encourage ethical reflection during fieldwork practice

Sarah Banks

Introduction

This chapter discusses the use of learning journals during fieldwork practice periods. It outlines the usefulness of a journal in developing students' skills in analysis and reflection, particularly in relation to ethical issues. It also considers some of the difficulties in using journals, drawn from the experience of students who participated in a recent research project in Durham and Copenhagen.

The reflective practitioner

In professional education and development the concept of the 'reflective practitioner' is regarded as important (see Banks, 2001, pp. 162-3; Schön, 1983, 1987; Smith, 1994; Wilde and Wilson, 2001). Moon (1999, p. 23) considers reflection as:

> A form of mental processing with a purpose and/or anticipated outcome that is applied to relatively complex or unstructured ideas for which there is not an obvious solution.

Given this definition, it is not hard to see how work on the ethical problems and dilemmas that arise in the everyday practice of the social professions can be used as a vehicle for reflection. Furthermore, skills in reflection are essential for students to be able to think through the complexities of the situations they encounter that have an ethical component.

Much of the literature on professional ethics stresses decision-making procedures – looking at how we come to make a good, balanced decision in a careful, rational way, taking into account ethical principles and rules and practical and technical features of a situation. This is an important skill, and is the subject of Chapters 6 and 7. However, the ability to reflect both 'in action' (while doing a task, or during an event or situation) and 'on action' (afterwards, looking back on the situation) is a vital prerequisite to making a good decision, and indeed for being a 'good' practitioner. It involves students developing an awareness of themselves and their role in a situation, an ability to ask why something happened, to question and make connections. It involves not taking things at 'face value' – that is, it involves digging beneath the surface. Students in their early years of professional education often find it hard to move beyond giving descriptive account of events (simply describing what happened) to offering reflective accounts, where the intention is to learn. Encouraging students to give verbal or written reflective accounts of situations involving ethical issues is a good way to encourage them to learn this skill.

Journals as a vehicle for reflection

Encouraging students to keep a reflective journal whilst they undertake periods of fieldwork practice is a way of developing their skills in reflective writing, and provides a basis for reflective discussion with their supervisors and fellow students. According to Carlsmith (1994):

> A journal is a cross between a diary (first person, subjective, personal) and a class notebook (third person, objective, filled with "facts"). It allows the student to combine his/her emotional reaction with an intellectual reaction, a process that will raise both the level of student interest and the quality of thought.

Through using a journal, students can be encouraged to think more clearly about difficult situations, reflect on their roles, what was happening and why. As Moon (1999, p. 4) comments in relation to learning journals in general:

A learning journal is essentially a vehicle for reflection. Probably all adults reflect, some more than others, and for those who do reflect, being reflective can represent a deeply seated orientation to their lives. For others, the process would seem to come about only when the conditions in their environment are conducive to reflecting, perhaps when there is an incentive to reflect, or some guidance or a particular accentuation of conditions. A learning journal represents an accentuation of those right conditions – some guidance, some encouragement, helpful questions or exercises and the expectation that journal writing can have a worthwhile consequence, whether at the end or within its process, or as a result of both.

We may be more familiar with idea of journals as personal diaries, where we record what we did each day (a 'log' or description). Sometimes our personal journals or diaries also include elements of reflection where we comment on what we did, make notes for self-improvement, and so on. The dividing lines between personal journals and those used in formal educational contexts, and between descriptive journals and learning journals, may not always be clear – and there is certainly some overlap. Even in the formal context of using learning journals in higher education, the language used is nevertheless more informal than that of the usual academic language. This relatively informal language, using the first person 'I', is termed 'expressive language', often used when we are in situations that are new, puzzling or intriguing. Moon suggests (1999, p. 30) that for many of us it comes in the form of 'scribbled notes, comments to ourselves and lines drawn between ideas'. What distinguishes a descriptive journal (where we simply describe what happened, either in a personal context or a formal learning situation) from a learning journal is the intention to learn. Hence any descriptive writing is included as a precursor to reflection. It may be a way of helping us sort out what happened, before then going on to consider why these things happened, what role we ourselves played, and so on (reflective writing). Moon (1999, p. 18) comments:

> Reflective writing could be likened to using the page as a meeting place in which ideas can intermingle and, in developing, give rise to new ideas for new learning.

Hatton and Smith (1995, quoted in Moon, p.103) offer a framework for recognising reflectivity in writing. It can be helpful for students to review their own journal writing in terms of this framework:

1. *Descriptive writing* – a description of events or literature reports. There is no discussion beyond description.
2. *Descriptive reflection* – description of events, plus some justification in relatively descriptive language. The possibility of alternative viewpoints in discussion is accepted. Reflection may be based generally on one perspective or factor as a rationale or, presumably in a more sophisticated form, is based on the recognition of multiple factors and perspectives.
3. *Dialogic reflection* – demonstrates a stepping back from the events and actions leading to a different level of mulling about discourse with oneself and exploring the discourse of events and actions. The reflection is analytical or integrative, linking factors and perspectives. It may reveal inconsistency in attempting to provide rationales and critiques.
4. *Critical reflection* – demonstrates an awareness that actions and events are not only located within and explicable by multiple perspectives, but are located in and influenced by multiple historical, ethical and socio-political contexts.

There are many other accounts of different stages or levels of reflectivity given in the literature (see Moon, pp. 100-104). Generally the more sophisticated forms of reflective writing ('critical reflection' in Hatton and Smith's list) are those that demonstrate understanding of the ethical, historical and socio-political context of the issue. For example, Van Manen's (1977) highest level of reflectivity includes 'incorporating consideration of moral and ethical criteria into discourse about practical action'. Sparkes-Langer and Colton (1991) include 'explanation with consideration of ethical, moral political issues' as the definition of their highest level of reflective thinking.

In research undertaken by Dart et al. (1998), most of their students produced writing gauged to be 'descriptive reflection'. Since we are wanting to work with students on the ethical issues arising in practice, we will inevitably be looking for them to go beyond descriptive reflection, to engage in dialogic and particularly critical reflection, which takes into account multiple perspectives of different people involved, different values and viewpoints, and locates the action/situation in both its particular context, and the broader socio-economic context. This does not mean that descriptive writing and descriptive reflection are not useful. They are, particularly as they help us understand what is going on in a situation and lead us on into deeper reflection.

The advantages of journal writing

Moon (1999, pp. 19-21) provides a useful list of ways in which journals help learning, of which the following is a summary:

1. *By demanding time and intellectual space* – journal writing forces you to stop and think.
2. *By encouraging independent learning and ownership of learning* – you have to be self-sufficient in deciding what you will write, and what you write has relevance for your own purpose.
3. *By providing a focussing point and an opportunity to order thoughts* – you can collect your thoughts and relate content to your own experience or previous knowledge.
4. *By the expression of emotion or affective function* – journal writing involves your feelings as well as your intellect, and so involves more of your whole 'persona' and is more lasting and pervasive.
5. *By dealing with situations that are not straightforward* – in our case, ethical issues are certainly not straightforward – there is no correct answer and the goal is to construct and defend reasonable solutions. King and Kitchener (1994, p. 11) speak of 'ill-structured' problems that 'cannot be described with a high degree of completeness', that 'cannot be resolved with a high degree of certainty' and where experts 'may disagree about the best solution, even when the problem can be considered solved'.
6. *By encouraging reflection* – following on from the above point, if you are asked to explain something or respond to a

thought-provoking question, you are likely to adopt a deep approach to learning (see Moon, 1999, p. 26) that requires the use of reflective processes.

7. *By improving capacities for 'metacognition'* – in thinking about how you learn, what stage you are at, reflecting on earlier entries in your journal, you develop the ability to monitor your own current state of learning (see Moon, 1999, p. 27).

8. *By developing writing skills and habits* – writing is an important means of learning (Moon, 1999, p. 29). As Richardson (1994, p. 517) comments:

> I write because I want to find something out. I write in order to learn something I didn't know before I wrote. I was taught, however, as perhaps you were too, not to write until I knew what I wanted to say, until my points were organised and outlined ….

Students in Durham and Copenhagen who kept learning journals during their fieldwork practice periods in 2001-2 reported that they found this experience very useful. The list of positive features of keeping a learning journal given below is compiled from a questionnaire given to second year students at the University of Durham in May 2002, who were halfway through their practice placement period:

- They journal is useful to refer to for academic work – for example, when referencing for written assignments;
- It enables you to reflect on things done;
- You can note things to be dealt with later;
- You can recap and relate to on-going issues;
- It is a way of processing and organizing information;
- It can be a way to unwind and make sense of feelings;
- You can look back and see high points and low points;
- You can bring the journal to supervision sessions;
- It helps you remember key issues and how you dealt with them;
- It helps you remember mistakes and enables you to learn from them;
- It helps you to follow up on action.

The challenges of journal writing

Although students reported that they found writing the journals useful, they also found it very challenging. The following are some of the difficulties noted by students and teachers in Durham and Copenhagen, with some suggestions for attempting to overcome them:

1. *Finding time and remembering to write in the journal* – it may be helpful to recommend to students that they set aside a period of time each day to write in their journals, and see this as a priority.
2. *Knowing what to write – how to select from experiences* – this capacity usually develops over time. It can be helpful for students to show some of their entries to their tutor or supervisor and discuss with them how they decide what is significant.
3. *Identifying ethical issues* – unless students have had some teaching on ethics before the placement, they may find it hard to identify what is an 'ethical issue' as distinct from professional practice issues in general. Some students report that all their work involves ethical issues, therefore it is difficult to select. Others may claim that no ethical issues arise (assuming an ethical issue is a big dilemma or conflict). Identification and analysis of the ethical issues in students' everyday practice requires a basic familiarity with a vocabulary and some key concepts (such as rights, duties, self-determination, welfare, justice and equality). Students may benefit from some input on ethical theory and professional codes of ethics prior to the placement period to enable them more easily to 'construct' the ethical issues in their practice.
4. *Finding a format that facilitates journal writing* – writing journal entries without using the structure of headings can encourage descriptive accounts; yet some students find using the headings (such as: 'description; analysis; action; reflection') too prescriptive. Different formats may be appropriate for different purposes or types of work. It may be helpful to encourage students to experiment, and to share their approaches with each other.

5. *Finding ways of expressing emotions* – many of the Durham students hardly mentioned their feelings or emotions in their journals. They may recognise the importance of including reference to emotions, as one student said: 'It may seem trivial if you don't put your emotions in'. But as another commented: 'It's hard to convey emotions. You can say: "they were really mad", but that doesn't convey how it was'.
6. *Achieving dialogic and critical reflection* – it can be useful to encourage students to re-read their journals regularly, perhaps even adding a regular 'reflective summary' at the end of each week. Reflecting after a week can enable the student to find some distance from events. Asking students specific questions and encouraging them to look critically at how they are using the journal may help.

Conclusions

Use of learning journals during fieldwork practice is valuable for encouraging reflection, planning and use in supervision and academic work. However, students using journals for the first time may require considerable support from their tutors, supervisors and fellow students in finding the time to keep the journal, finding the best format and working out how to be analytical and reflective. It could be beneficial for students to practise keeping a journal and get feedback on this before they undertake their fieldwork placements. If the journal is to be used to record and analyse ethical issues and dilemmas experienced by the students during their fieldwork practice, they will benefit from some input on how to identify the ethical dimensions of situations and a familiarity with a basic conceptual framework.

Acknowledgements

I am grateful to Birgitte Møller and the participating students of the University of Durham and Københavns Socialpædagogiske Seminarium for their input into a small research project on using journals in fieldwork practice, the results of which have been used in this chapter. The Durham part of the research was funded by the University of Durham Research and Development in Learning and Teaching Research Grants Scheme.

Appendix 4.1:
Using a learning journal during fieldwork practice

An example of guidelines for students

(adapted from guidelines developed for use by the Community and Youth Work Studies Unit, University of Durham).

Students are required to keep a placement journal to help maximise their learning during the fieldwork practice. A journal provides repeated opportunities for skilled observation and reflection in a structured format, and offers a framework for the systematic gathering, recording and analysis of information for use in meeting the written work requirements of the placement. Particular points to note about the placement journal are:

1) *The journal as evidence of practice development* – the journal is an important element of a successful placement and provides evidence that you have developed personally and professionally in your practice. Over time it will show how your understanding, skills and confidence have developed. It will also help you identify areas of weakness for your future training needs.

2) *The journal as a planning tool* – the journal is a useful tool for preparing, planning and recording work sessions in detail. The journal can also be used to prepare for supervision sessions and course tutor visits, and to record your reflections on these events.

3) *The journal as a personal record* – the journal itself does not have to be shown to the fieldwork tutor/supervisor, although extracts can be used in supervision sessions, if helpful.

4) *Handing in the journal* – you will be asked to hand in your placement journal along with your final placement report to demonstrate that you have used a journal. It may be read by tutors or external examiners. You may remove sections you do not wish to be read.

5) *The journal and your placement reports* – the journal itself is not formally assessed, but you will be asked to submit selected recordings drawn from your journal to support your written work as a record of incidents, conversations, interventions or impressions.

How to keep your journal

The journal can be used as a detailed log to gather facts and observations – such as information about the agency and how it works; information about what sessions/work you have been involved with, what happened and who was there. It should also include your analysis of and reflections on facts, information and observations – such as why there is misunderstanding in the agency management committee; what went wrong at a residential event; what ethical issues were raised; what you have learnt about how to handle conflict. How you use it may vary according to the type of placement and your own needs. It might include:

- *a basic diary of events* – a brief descriptive record of what you did/what happened each day;
- *detailed recordings of particularly difficult/interesting events/situations* – stories about a particular person, event, situation with details of who did what, how people felt, what happened, why it mattered;
- *future planning* – a recording, plus explanations and plans for action;
- *reflections* – comments on your developing role as a student practitioner; 'feelings'; controversial or ethical issues; evaluative notes about the usefulness of interventions; what you are learning.

There is no pre-set format for the journal. The journal is your own, and therefore you can decide what format it takes and how you structure it. Here are some suggestions about how to keep your journal:

- *Use a loose leaf ring binder*, dedicated to the journal.
- *Number the pages.*

- *Create an ongoing table of contents.*
- *Re-read your entries*, and add further comments and reflections. You may need to add in an extra page. Highlight interesting or important bits. Add new sections or make annotations.
- *Write weekly summaries/reflections* – re-reading the journal every week can be very beneficial, as can writing reflections on the week's events – reflecting on your role, noting developing difficulties or resolutions of issues, planning future action, noting learning, significant changes in attitudes of oneself or others, any ethical issues. A loose leaf format facilitates the adding in of comments and reflections.
- *Reflect on your use of the journal* (perhaps also weekly) – how descriptive, analytical or reflective are you? Are you noting your emotions? How easy or difficult do you find it to write? Is it developing your skills in recording, analysing and reflecting? What are you using it for?

Section on ethical issues and dilemmas

Students are asked to keep a special section of their journal for reflections on ethical issues and dilemmas. In this section it would be appropriate to write several short case study descriptions of situations raising ethical issues for you and your analysis of how and why these arose, how you felt about the situation, what you decided to do and why (see the task for the recall day). You might reflect on any discussions you have with your fieldwork tutor or colleagues, and how these influence your views about the situation. You might also reflect on your own values as a professional worker, and how these are being challenged or developing over the course of the placement.

Reflective recordings

One of the main aims of the journal is to encourage your reflection on your experiences and your actions whilst on placement, and hence to encourage learning. This can be regarded as a cyclical process, as shown in Figure 4.1 below.

Figure 4.1: Fieldwork Practice Learning Cycle
(adapted from Reece and Walker, 2000)

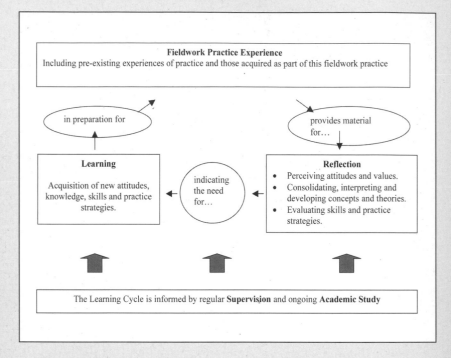

Jennifer Moon (1999), in her book on learning journals (*Learning Journals: A Handbook for Academics, Students and Professional Development*, London, Kogan Page, pp. 85 ff.) offers the following advice about the process of writing reflectively:

- Make the journal your own;
- Be honest;
- Let words flow;
- Use your own words – be informal;
- Dig deeper;
- Be flexible;
- Write things up as soon as you can;
- Seek help if necessary;
- Be selective.

Example of recordings

The example below (based on a student undertaking fieldwork practice in a community centre) gives an idea of what a detailed recording of a particular situation, event or piece of work might look like – initially recording your observations, analysis of events and your proposed course of action. The aim is to build skills in observation, analysis and action processes. Over time your recordings of work with individuals and groups will provide a good basis for you to see how your first impressions, analysis and actions have changed. You might then like to go back to recordings you made several weeks ago and reflect on them.

12/3/03

Observation *(description of what happened)*
Yet another afternoon when the men's group totally dominated the space. They created a lot of disruption by their noisy laughter from a game of table football. They also interfered with other groups in the centre, by wandering around and making threatening comments – particularly targeting the girls and women.

John B seems to be the centre of things but the rest of them seem to egg him on. He went up to Tracy, who was in a meeting in the coffee bar to plan the carnival, and made derogatory comments about her organisational skills. The other young men then joined in and started to mock the whole idea of the carnival. I was with the carnival planning group and just told John to go away – he hung around for a bit and then they went back to the table football.

Analysis/reflection *(explaining what happened and reflecting on what it means)*
I know that they've been neglected lately because of staff shortages. It could be that it is attention seeking. They've also been together in the centre for about two years and they give the impression of owning the place.

Wonder if John is the leader or the one that fires the bullets?

It could be they don't realise that they are harassing the women and we may have been lax in keeping the equal opportunities policy on the agenda. Suspect the women and girls just accept it as the norm but it could de-motivate them. Ethical issues: rights of women and girls to space and freedom from harassment; equality of opportunity and fairness in use of resources.

I told John to go away, but didn't do anything more, as I wasn't sure how they would react and felt it was more important to get on with the meeting. But was I chickening out? Ethical issue: what is my professional duty here? Ought I to have challenged the young men more directly?

Action (notes of what you need to do/bear in mind)
1. I must find a way of letting them know in no uncertain terms that being so dominating and harassing the women is not acceptable. Check agency policy for sanctions in case they are necessary.
2. Discuss with Sue (women's worker) to see if she thinks there's a need for coordinated work.
3. Work more closely with the group – try to find out how they relate to each other and get to know John as an individual.
4. Focus work on trying to get them to plan and implement more useful things to do with their time.
5. Discuss this group with my fieldwork tutor in next supervision session.

29/4/03

Further reflections on this incident
I think I felt quite uncertain what to do at this point – not able to act until I knew what the agency policy was and had talked to other people. This was partly because as a student I felt insecure, and also because I didn't know the young men very well, and hadn't been working directly with them. As my later recordings show, I have started to do some work with these young men, and have also worked out how to tackle their disruptive behaviour as soon as it starts. The ethical dimensions of this situation were very much to do with my responsibility as a worker to challenge harassment and to ensure all individuals and groups get a fair share of available resources.

Recall days

There are two 'recall days' (days when students come in to the University from their full-time fieldwork practice period) held at the University. The aims of a recall day are to assist the students in reflecting on their fieldwork practice experience and to offer opportunities for support from tutors and fellow students. Each student is asked to prepare a written account of a situation they have encountered in their practice, with copies for their fellow students. These situations are discussed in turn in small groups of about eight students led by tutors over a two hour period. Care must be taken to respect individuals and organisations by anonymising identifying details (particularly names), or seeking any necessary permission to use information.

The task for the first recall day involves writing about an ethical issue as follows:

Preparation Task: Description and analysis of an ethical issue

Think of an event or situation that raised/is raising ethical issues for you. This might be a situation you found/are finding problematic, conflictual, and/or where it was/is difficult to make a decision. Issues of rights, duties, human welfare, fairness, justice or equality may be involved.

1. *Briefly describe what happened* (the key events, people, circumstances);
2. *Identify the ethical issues involved* and comment on them (for example, in the example of a recording given earlier, issues might include: women's rights to space and freedom from harassment; equality of opportunity; fairness in the use of resources; professional duties and responsibilities).
3. *Reflections*
   a) Reflect on what action was taken and/or could have been taken. Why was it taken? What could have been done differently?
   b) Reflect on your role and your emotions.
   c) Reflect on what you have learnt from analysing and reflecting on this situation/event.

5.
Using Socratic dialogue

Frank Philippart

Introduction

Socratic dialogue is a method of practical reasoning that can usefully be applied to ethical issues and questions of values and norms in the social professions. In this chapter I will draw on my experience of using Socratic dialogue as part of a training programme for social workers in the Netherlands. Socratic dialogue gives professional workers the opportunity to think through ethical issues and develop insights into values and norms they choose to put into practice.

Using Socratic dialogue in social education

Education for practitioners in the social professions should aim to enable them to deal with ethical issues and ethical decision-making in their daily practice. Perhaps it is superfluous to say this, but frequently we tend to believe that teaching theory makes for better practice. In the case of our ethical behaviour, in the immediacy of professional working there is often a gap between our theoretical knowledge and our actions.

Speaking of ethics and competencies in the social professions, we need to focus on the development of 'ethical awareness' in addition to knowledge, skills and attitudes. In the teaching of ethics in professional education, we need to consider how we can work on developing ethical awareness, other than by hoping it will develop by itself once our students engage in practice. In most cases it will develop, but in some cases it may not.

Starting with these questions, some years ago at Hogeschool Brabant in the Netherlands we began a search for a method to help integrate knowledge, skills and attitudes in the field of ethics. The aim was to develop the competence of social professionals in dealing with ethical dilemmas in the reality of their daily work. Socratic dialogue, a particular method of questioning taken-for-granted assumptions, proved to be very useful to this end. Nelson and Kessels (1994) and van Hooft (2001a, 2001b) give useful outlines of this approach. In the Netherlands, Kessels (1997) has written several books and engaged in training professionals to work with the method of Socratic dialogue.

The origins of Socratic dialogue

The method of Socratic dialogue has its origins in the dialogues of Socrates and in Plato's writings on these dialogues. The dialogues have resulted in Socrates being considered as one of the founding thinkers of western philosophy, although he never wrote down his insights in textbooks. Socrates had a rigorous way of raising fundamental questions in dialogues with fellow citizens. In these dialogues he addressed core issues by systematically asking questions of people who were considered to be experts on the subject. He analysed these questions in a systematic way in the course of a dialogue. For Socrates, the way in which people address these questions in everyday life was the source and goal of his philosophical reasoning. In this way Socrates became a teacher, through searching for the practical ideas that govern people's behaviour.

Today we live in a 'postmodern', pluralistic, differentiated and multi-cultural society. Many conflicting interests, interpretations of reality, moral and ethical standards, visions and hopes for the future exist next to each other. Socratic dialogue proves very useful for the exploration of the ethical dilemmas and conflicts that arise in this melting pot. Socratic dialogue helps constitute a growing awareness of the actual assumptions, presuppositions, norms and values that play a role in the personal and collective thinking and feeling on very different kinds of matters. This helps workers in the social professions to become clear on the ways to approach difficult questions and ethical dilemmas that can not be answered easily.

Some examples of questions to be addressed with Socratic dialogue

Socratic dialogue deals with questions. An example of such a question might be: 'Should the social worker support or oppose the deeply-felt wish of a couple with learning disabilities to have a child, knowing that they can never take adequate care of children?' Another example of a question is: 'Should the social worker help an illegal immigrant even when this puts the social worker and his/her organisation in a difficult position in that it would involve breaking the law?' An interesting question for the social professions is: 'Where do we draw the line between self-determination and interference and why specifically at one point rather than another?'

Why Socratic dialogue in the education for the social professions?

The social professions have to address these and many other ethical questions that arise in modern society. Working in the social professions becomes increasingly complicated as society itself becomes more complex. In recent years our professional education has been reoriented from knowledge-based and teacher-centred to competence-based and student-centred. In the end we want our students to have the ability to make decisions in this rapidly changing, multicultural society. In line with these changes we need to rethink the ways in which ethical decisions are made.

Socratic dialogue helps constitute an awareness that is focused on finding consensus on principles, values and ideas. This awareness is essential for addressing the problems of modern society, where monologues and the production of yet more rules do not provide solutions. Furthermore, Socratic dialogue helps in the development of a critical attitude towards cultural and societal developments and the discovery of contradictions and paradoxes in social behaviour.

How does Socratic dialogue work?

Socratic dialogue is, as explained above, a rigorous inquiry into a question and our own thinking and feeling about it. The dialogue aims to encourage the investigation of assumptions in a joint process. In the end we may find there are two outcomes: shared insight and an answer to the question, preferably in the form of a consensus. The dialogue is best practised in a group of two to eight people, but can even be used in groups up to a hundred or more people in a somewhat modified form. In this form it is regularly performed in so-called 'Socratic cafés'. Perhaps we can say that the larger the group, the more difficult it gets to come to a deeper level of understanding, but of course this also depends on the participants in the group.

In Socratic dialogue a general question or issue is explored by questioning personal experience and common beliefs. The participants share a common interest in exploring a question. Characteristic to Socratic dialogue is that the question is explored through analysing practical experience: the exploration of assumptions, concepts and beliefs that underlie the common, practised behaviour. From there we go deeper into the 'hows', 'whys' and 'wherefores'. Personal experience (in relation to the question) is made concrete in a particular example that is shared by a participant in order to throw light on the question. The participant who chooses to give the example is called the 'answer-giver' and is questioned about the exact reasons, motives and background of their action or behaviour in relation to the example they have given. This procedure is also known as 'regressive abstraction'. Elaborating on a question, we start with an example in which the concept is initiated and from there we start looking for the more abstract and general assumptions and eventually principles lying at the basis of this example – reasoning from the particular example to the abstract principles.

The hourglass procedure

To make this 'regressive abstraction' work, the Socratic dialogue follows a set of logically connected steps in the 'hourglass' procedure (see Figure 5.1) as follows:

1. *Choose a question* – The first step is to agree upon a well-formulated philosophical question as a focus point for the dialogue. The question or statement should be answerable

by thinking about it (rather than with reference to general empirical data) and agreed upon by the participants. An example might be:

> *To what extent may you interfere with someone's behaving or acting when you think that it is better for that person's well-being?*

This example is drawn from a dialogue with students. The elaborations that follow are used merely as an illustration of the different steps in a dialogue. For readability the example is kept short and simple. In reality Socratic dialogue follows much higher standards of elaboration.

2. *Collect concrete examples* – The next step is to collect concrete examples from participants' own experience in which the given topic plays a key role. For instance, one student gave this example:

> *My friend, after having drunk too much alcohol, refused to listen to my advice and wanted to get into his car and drive home. Then I decided to take away his car keys, so that he couldn't drive away.*

To ensure that everyone has a commitment to the dialogue, it is advisable to have examples from every participant.

3. *Choose an example* – One of the examples is chosen by the group as the basis of analysis and argumentation throughout the dialogue. The 'owner' of the example then acts as 'answer-giver' in exploring the motives and background underlying the concrete actions.

4. *Formulate a 'key assertion'* – The other participants ask questions in such manner that the essence of the given example is understood. This common understanding that all participants finally agree upon is formulated as a so-called 'key-assertion'. This is essentially a provisional answer to the original question. In our example the question was: 'To what extent …?' After some questioning the participants agreed upon the following key assertion:

> *Interference with decisions people make is allowed to the extent that I should do everything I can to protect someone from harming themselves and/or others, when they are not capable of doing this themselves.*

5. ***Formulating rules and principles*** – From here, through
   regressive abstraction, the more abstract and general
   assumptions and principles on which the concrete action is
   based are elaborated. A lot of questions can be asked about
   the 'hows', 'whys' and 'wherefores' of the statement given
   above. In this example, other values such as 'freedom of
   choice' and the value of 'self-determination' are violated in
   favour of values like 'care' and 'safety'. What rules govern
   the decision to interfere? What rules lead to the opposite
   decision, that is: not to interfere? What principles legitimate
   the rules? In the above example, a rule might be formulated
   as follows:

   *When a person's ability consciously to exercise freedom of will is
   hampered (that is, under the influence of alcohol), and they threat-
   en to do things they would not do under normal circumstances,
   then you may consider acting yourself in the interests of their well-
   being, by interfering.*

   Of course, this so-called 'rule' may engender many new
   problems, but this should be considered as an advantage of
   the method of Socratic dialogue. It tends to raise more fundamental questions up to the level where the participants
   reach consensus on the 'solid ground' of rules and principles that can be widely applied.

6. ***Recording of key statements*** – Crucial statements made by
   participants should be written down on a flipchart or board,
   so that all participants can have an overview and be clear
   about the sequence of the discourse. For example, in the
   orienting phase of the dialogue, this statement might be
   recorded:

   *I took away his keys, because I felt responsible. If I had let him
   drive away, and something had happened, then I would have
   blamed myself for not having interfered …*

The process of 'regressive abstraction' is symbolised in the
form of the hourglass: the top half of the hour-glass is funnel-
shaped, indicating that the philosophical question is narrowed
down to a concrete example known by experience by one of
the participants in the dialogue. This example is further nar-

rowed down to a key assertion that is taken as the provisional answer to the question that the example-giver expressed in the praxis of the experience by acting in a certain way. The lower half of the hourglass is cone-shaped, indicating that from there we start looking for more general rules that the example-giver followed in deciding to act in the manner expressed in the example. The aim of the dialogue is to arrive at a clear understanding of the general principles and values that underlie our behaviour. These last two phases are a broadening and deepening of the dialogue. The exploration of the rules and principles transcends the particularity of this one example and this one person to more general rules and principles underlying our choices of behaviour. The rules and principles that give direction – and meaning – to our behaviour have a more general character in certain cultural contexts and are common to groups of people and not only to the particular person in this particular example.

Figure 5.1: The hourglass procedure

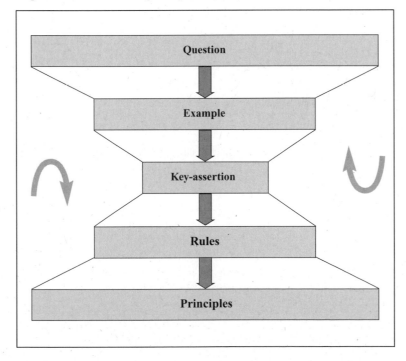

The procedure involves moving back and forth between the different levels to check if certain conclusions are in line with the given example. This may entail moving from question to example; from key-assertion to example and question; from rules to key-assertions to example. This moving back and forth in the argumentation also gives the participants the opportunity to reach consensus on ethical rules and principles, and discuss the ways they wish to apply them, especially in cases of ethical dilemmas. The model aims at reaching consensus and helps to develop a clearer sense of ethical reasoning. Anyone at any time can start another dialogue on a new example or addressing new circumstances, thus deepening our understanding and commitment to the ethical rules and principles we use.

A Socratic dialogue, exercised in this way, can last from a few hours to several days. In the example mentioned above, the hourglass procedure for one of the many possible lines of reasoning is depicted in Figure 5.2

Figure 5.2: The hourglass procedure in practice

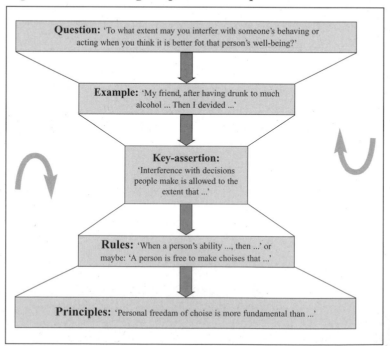

Starting a dialogue

Finally I want to give some indications of how to formulate a question and start a Socratic dialogue. Some points to note about the initial question are that it should be:

- general, not purely individual;
- fundamental;
- relevant, motivating, of interest to the participants;
- answerable by philosophical reasoning (not empirical);
- simply formulated;
- of such a form that there is the possibility of giving concrete examples.

It is important to formulate a specific question (and not to settle for a general subject for discussion) because it helps focus on the issue, making it more pronounced and concrete. By formulating a question, a space is created for questioning and exploration in which a mutual interest is created instead of directly trying to solve the issue raised.

Some examples of questions are:

- What is integrity in behaviour?
- To what extent are you responsible for all the people that are under your care?
- To what extent is a person responsible for the consequences of their actions?
- When do you stop helping?
- To what extent may you interfere with someone's behaving or acting when you think that it is better for that person's well-being?

In relation to the last question, one of my students responded with this example:

> One of the people I work with is an under-aged girl of sixteen years, who ran away from home to live with her boyfriend, a 22 year-old man. In one of our meetings she told me, confidentially, that this man put pressure on her to pay for her maintenance by prostitution. At this point I decided to interfere, even when it was against her will.

When I feel that someone isn't able to make a free and conscious choice for the well-being of herself, I can intervene, even if the person doesn't agree.

The starting point of the Socratic dialogue is an example. Each participant brings to the dialogue an example in which a choice or action is made in relation to the question or the key concept. In the above question, issues of 'integrity', 'responsibility' and 'helping' are instantiated. In the student's example, the presumed right to interfere was questioned. After some or all examples have been heard, the group chooses one to be the subject of the enquiry on the basis of the criteria that the example should be:

* Drawn from our experience (not hypothetical);
* Relevant to all participants;
* Recognisable as an example of the question to all participants;
* Active – that is, the example-giver has participated themselves by acting, or by taking a certain position or point of view on it or having made a judgement;
* Finished – that is, the experience has come to an end;
* Not unduly complicated;
* One where the example-giver is willing to provide additional information to the group so they can investigate it fully;
* Motivating for the other participants.

The next step is that the 'owner' of the chosen example or case is asked to tell it in full, with all the details, thoughts and feelings that are considered relevant. Then the other participants explore the given example by asking for the facts and also for the ideas that played a role in the example. Participants should try to get a clear and vivid picture of the given example or case. All participants should be able to picture themselves in the situation of the example-giver. This stage ends with the formulating of one or more 'key assertions'. Participants should ask themselves: 'Is this the point that has to be made?' or 'Is this the issue that it all turns on?' They should connect the example and key assertions to the initial question, asking what meaning the concepts involved in the question have in the given example. It is important to define the concepts in a specific and concrete manner. This is the middle phase of the hourglass procedure.

The group in the anecdote decided on the following as the key assertion in the given example:

> *When I feel that someone isn't able to make a free and conscious choice for the well-being of herself, I can intervene, even if the person doesn't agree.*

Needless to say, a number of participants in the dialogue-group would never have decided on such a drastic move. From here you start looking for presuppositions or justifications of the key assertion: 'How did you come to think ....?', 'Why do you think that ...?', 'Is this what made you act in this way?' The questioning from there pointed to:

> What is the basis for that 'right to intervene'? How do you know when to intervene and when a person is able to decide for herself? Did the young age of your client play a role in your decision to intervene? How do you think about prostitution? How fundamental is a young person's right to self-determination? And what about a person's freedom? When do you think the person can decide for themselves?

It is then important to test the justifications, by questioning their validity and asking what the others would do in this situation. Students can be asked on what grounds they think that the given arguments are valid, and whether this is sufficient reason to act in a certain way. The facilitator should then seek consensus on the justifications and key assertion, asking if this is the answer to the initial question. It is also useful to make notes of the sequence of the whole dialogue and to summarize the main arguments and justifications, including the points on which consensus is achieved and the new questions that arose out of this.

General conditions

In Socratic dialogue there are some additional rules or conditions to be met, to make sure that the dialogue can unfold freely:

- It is important to make sure that participants' contributions are based upon what they have experienced, not upon what they have read or heard;
- Strive for consensus;
- Try to understand the thoughts of the other participants; postpone your (pre-) judgements;
- Express yourself clearly and concisely;
- Think for yourself (make no appeals to authority); express your actual doubts but not hypothetical ones.

The three levels of dialogue

There are three levels of dialogue that should be clearly distinguished:

1. The first level is that of the content dialogue – the level at which the question is addressed.
2. The second level is that of the strategic dialogue – the level at which questions of procedure are dealt with (for instance, asking for a decision on the direction in which the dialogue should proceed, because you feel that certain arguments are sufficiently looked into).
3. The third level is that of the meta dialogue – the level at which matters of group behaviour and feeling are handled (for instance, asking for a tea-break because you are getting hungry).

Keeping these levels separate allows the content dialogue to proceed untroubled by other considerations.

The training in Socratic dialogue

Training for Socratic dialogue is given in the first year of a four-year educational programme and is part of a course on philosophical reasoning and the fundamentals of theory and practice in social work. The method of Socratic dialogue is repeatedly applied in several courses throughout the four-year educational programme as one of the ways in which students can work with presented cases and dilemmas. In the third year, it is used in a course on professional autonomy and accountability in relation to law, theory and ethics. The students find it very interesting and rewarding, once they succeed in having an actual Socratic dialogue that shows results. In the beginning it takes some time to train the students in the workings of Socratic dialogue. The most difficult point is to persist in exploring the issue and not to fall into a debate on the advantages and disadvantages of certain points of view. In the Socratic dialogue we are, on the contrary, very interested in the deeper basis for certain ways of thinking in terms of rules, values and principles that guide a person's thinking and acting. Students find it difficult to get accustomed to the higher levels of disciplined thinking and reasoning that are required in the method and to stay focused during the course of a dialogue. It takes students about four sessions to get accustomed to the technique and really start using it in a meaningful way. From that point, repeated practice begins to contribute to a growing awareness of ethical and philosophical reasoning. Students then start to address issues they find interesting or challenging themselves.

In addition to giving students an initial training in Socratic dialogue, we introduce a number of basic themes in philosophy and in social work. Each theme forms the subject matter for one week in which the students study on the subject, try to formulate their own questions and try to discover the ethical issues in relation to the subject in the field of social work. At the end of the week the subject is discussed in the group and the questioning and different points of view are expressed and argued about with reference to the texts that have been studied. Each week we decide on an issue or question we want to explore in more depth and that question becomes the key to a Socratic dialogue session. How this works is explained below. The message is that any question is worth exploring in an open and thoughtful manner.

The subjects that are addressed in this particular programme are very common and fundamental for every practitioner in the social professions:

- Happiness and wisdom;
- Values and norms;

- Human relations;
- Thinking and feeling;
- Freedom and predestination;
- Responsibility and guilt;
- Justice and society.

In the programme the students study philosophical, sociological and historical elaborations on these subjects. In workshops the students receive an initial training in the method of Socratic dialogue and practice the method to explore their own values and ideas and those of their fellows on all the different subjects. Motivating questions are agreed upon with the students and subsequently worked through. The result is that students develop a more integrated vision of their professional role in society.

Conclusions

Socratic dialogue is a useful way of encouraging students to become aware of the ethical dimensions of their work, explore their own values and develop skills in critical thinking and argument. In the dialogical process, students have to work together to explore a question and formulate rules and principles, and so it develops their skills in listening, expressing their ideas and in reaching consensus. With its emphasis on analysis, reasoning and the formulation of rules and principles, it may have a tendency to reinforce principle-based approaches to ethics (see Chapter 1). However, because the examples are rooted in personal experience, the method does allow for (and can even encourage) the taking into account of emotions, feelings, personal qualities and relationships. The use of Socratic dialogue does, however, require a substantial commitment on the part of both the students and the teacher. It needs preparation (training for both the teacher and students) and a reasonably long period of time to complete a dialogue. Although it is not necessary to carry on a dialogue over several days, this can be a valuable experience.

6.

Working with a staged plan

Henk Goovaerts

Introduction

This chapter outlines a seven stage process that can be used as
a framework for analysing and discussing ethical problems and
dilemmas. A particular case is taken as a starting point, and
used to demonstrate the kinds of questions and issues that
could be considered at each stage.

However, a staged plan is only a tool, the effectiveness of
which lies in the quality of communication between the partners in the discussion.

Ethical choices and reflective competence

At the foundation of every action we perform as a practitioner
in the social professions, there lies a whole range of intentions
of which we can be aware, to some degree. These include goals
as well as motivations, both of which may differ between
individuals, even if they are performing the same action. We
can and must assess these motivations, goals and consequences
of actions, not only from a strictly professional point of view,
but also from an ethical perspective. Professional and ethical
criteria should always go together in social work. It is typical
of ethical judgement that we start thinking about the 'humane'
nature of the action. We ask ourselves: 'To what extent does
the action boost the ethical quality of life of the people
involved?' An action that is correct from a professional point
of view is not always ethical.

At this point, the discussion is obviously about what is ethical and about what criteria we should use. In the search for

answers to these questions, we put ourselves in the middle of the ethical discussion. Some of us would call an action 'good' if it is an expression of respect for a number of rights of the people involved, such as the right to privacy and participation. Others might emphasize the honest course of action, and so on.

When you face a situation in which there are several choices ranging from 'good and feasible' to 'not so good and easy', or when you have to choose between several good and bad solutions, then you have an ethical problem. People tend to have different opinions, depending on their professional training, their personal and family backgrounds, their position in the organisation or their own nature or character. Therefore, it is essential in any form of education to stimulate professional practitioners to reflect on ethical problems. As Sommer (1993) states, living in a hyper-modern reality means that education as the 'distribution of knowledge' is changing. This in turn requires a reorientation and creates new challenges for the education of social professionals in decisive ways, including:

- Expertise is regarded as an 'eternal' process of inquiring;
- A movement from one-dimensional to multi-dimensional understanding in the education of social workers;
- A movement from a stress on the social worker-as-a-role towards the social worker-as-a-person;
- The importance of practical embodied knowledge of everyday life in different contexts;
- A stress on reflective competence.

This reflective competence is essential in the discussion about a 'good' solution, and a staged plan can serve as a foothold to achieve this 'good' solution. When you are struggling with an ethical problem, it is important to know what to think of and what to take into account when making a choice.

Starting with a case

When teaching professional ethics in the training programme for social care workers at the Katholieke Hogeschool Limburg in Belgium, I always begin with 'the case of Alice'. With this case I try to explore and concretise the problematic nature of an ethical discussion:

> *The case of Alice* – Alice is the 16 year-old only daughter of divorced parents. When she was eight years old, her parents broke up after a rather violent relationship. Initially Alice was living with her mother, but this soon went wrong because of her mother's changing partners. She moved to her father's house, but he could not give her the time and attention she needed because of his work. At the age of 12, Alice was living on the streets most of the time and there was absolutely no supervision of her comings and goings. She quickly started skipping school and came into contact with drugs. She started sniffing glue and got involved in some minor shoplifting cases. Her parents were confronted with her behaviour, but at that time the contact between them and Alice was so bad that she was admitted into residential care.
>
> Despite the efforts of the couple in the residential home to give 14 year-old Alice some family affection and a daily routine, she withdrew into herself more and more and grew deeply suspicious of all adults. Because of a few incidents, including a small fire, Alice could not stay in the home any longer, and the juvenile court put her into a semi-open institution for 14 to 18 year-old girls. She has been in the community for six months now, and it has been going fairly well. There are fewer incidents, but people worry most about what is going on inside Alice's mind. She does not unwind and she is very shy. She regularly practises self-mutilation on her arms and legs and feels a lot of hatred and distress inside.
>
> The staff team working in the institution is self-managed and consists of a number of experienced people who have agreed to comply with certain principles regarded as vitally important, including:
>
> - Decisions are made collectively and in consensus;
> - Once a month, intensive peer-supervision by an external person takes place, during which the focus is on one of the team members;
> - No secrets are kept from each other; everything can be discussed.
>
> One day, Alice walks up to George, the youngest and most recently hired care worker, and asks him if he has a little time to spare for her. At the beginning of their conversation, Alice says that she has a serious problem she would like to discuss with him, because she has the impression that she can trust him, but that he cannot tell the others about it. George is rather hesitant in his response, and reminds her of

the agreement in the team. Alice clams up and mutters: 'I should have known!'

- What does George do now? or What will George have to do now?
- What choices does George have to make, taking into account, on the one hand, his loyalty towards his team and, on the other, Alice's question?
- What would you do?

The students are given the task of reflecting on this case in groups. Quite soon there turn out to be two camps, namely: those who resolutely choose for the team and those who choose for Alice. Several advantages and disadvantages are considered and one group often tries hard to convince the other that they are right. I often see students getting stuck in this 'dilemma': they often only give one or two options, to be quickly brought back to the essence of the problem by the others: the choice between the team or Alice.

Apparently, students seem to have some difficulty in exploring such a problem in a broader context and in realising that their solutions sometimes have more to do with their own intentions and expectations than with what Alice really needs. Nor do the students succeed in distancing themselves from the problem in order to find alternatives, because they often mix emotional arguments with rational ones. Later, after having studied the staged plan, I ask the students to look at the problem again, and this produces quite a number of surprising analyses.

Using a staged plan

Several authors have given instructions as to the steps to be taken to come to a well-balanced opinion and decision. The process usually involves asking yourself a number of important questions, to which answers need to be found before taking a decision. To take all important factors into account, you have to answer the questions one by one. Such a staged plan is a practical aid and does not automatically provide any standard solutions. It prevents you from rushing into things or from doing things you will regret later on. It forces people to strip problems in which they are emotionally involved of their tension, by systematically analysing them from different angles.

Moreover, with such a plan, you can explain to others why you have taken a particular decision. It makes you answerable to yourself for your own actions. Thus, people are forced explicitly to put into words and to justify a number of choices they usually make from a personal or professional point of view and which often remain unspoken. This gives a clear indication of how you have handled your freedom and responsibility. At the same time, a staged plan like this also offers you a structure in which decisions are taken together with other people, because at work you do not take important decisions on your own, but as a team. It takes quite a lot of deliberation and discussion.

I would suggest a six-stage plan that ends with an assessment of the whole process. The staged plan presented below is based on several other staged plans I found in the literature including those of Ebskamp and Kroon (1990), De Jonghe (1995) and especially Houdart (1997).

On the whole, the staged plan I will present here is similar to the one Houdart describes. However, I emphasize more strongly the alternatives in stage 4 and, within these alternatives, the creativity of the people involved. To my mind, you can thus avoid 'dilemma-thinking' (focusing on two mutually exclusive choices) and encourage the participants to search for alternatives with an open mind. This has several advantages, including:

- it creates new solutions, which did not exist previously;
- it stimulates participants to reflect freely and openly;
- it offers opponents the opportunity to find a solution without 'losing' the argument;
- it offers new opportunities for social work;
- it has an emancipatory effect because it allows everybody to participate in their own way.

Finally, I would like to point out that, in order to have a satisfactory ethical discussion, several preconditions have to be fulfilled. In this case 'satisfactory' does not mean 'ideal' or 'unanimous', but rather a discussion that all participants can live with; that is a discussion that invites people to move on.

An essential precondition is to be able and willing to speak freely, while a second precondition is that participants know which decisions they can and can not make. Houdart (1997) describes these preconditions as stage zero, which seems logical, given that compliance with these conditions is a 'conditio sine qua non'. However, I would not put it so strongly, because this issue is usually assessed during the course of the discussion and only then can it be tackled. I rather agree with the premise used in Theme Centred Interaction (TCI): 'Disturbances have priority' (Cohn, 1976).

After stage 6, I have added the assessment stage. This is a necessary stage, but it does not have to be performed immediately. Indeed it is often more fruitful if there is some 'time to reflect' before tackling stage 7.

The seven stage plan

The different stages in this plan are:

Stage 1: What are the facts?
It is advisable to approach the situation as objectively as possible, because it will enable you to get a clear view of the situation. This often does not work when you are emotionally involved. In that case, you need outsiders to help brush aside prejudices and opinions when all the facts are listed relating to questions of: 'who, what, why, where, when and how?' You need to consider which facts (old and new ones) are necessary? Are they reliable, relevant and complete? Of course, it is about gathering this factual knowledge according to ability and circumstances. Most of the time you only have little material and limited time. Furthermore, it is important to objectify as much as possible the rather subjective information to give participants the chance to look upon the problem from a meta-level – to take, as it were, an aerial view. In relation to the case of Alice, these questions might be considered:

> What facts with regard to Alice's past and present can we list and from whom did we get this information? Is it important to gain insight into the subjective perception of this information and consider whether you need to discuss it with Alice?

Stage 2: Whose interests are at stake?

This analysis can give rise to a confusion of interests. Under 'interest' we understand: that which meets someone's needs; is advantageous to someone; is, deservedly or undeservedly, good for someone. This stage involves trying to gain insight into the people involved in the dilemma and discovering the meaning of their interests and opinions. In other words: how do the people involved experience the facts, how do they think and feel about them? After all, everyone involved in social work has a number of responsibilities for the effective performance of the job. It is quite possible that what is being presented as a particular 'interest' is also linked with someone's responsibilities in social work. In other words, who is responsible for what? It is often about weighing up the values, whether or not connected with certain interests. At this stage, you try to get clarity and come to a conclusion regarding the nature of the real problem, for example:

> In Alice's situation, her interests have priority, but to what extent do George's or other team members' interests come into play? Does the whole team have an interest in a particular choice with regard to the organisation? Who bears the real responsibility in a self-directed team, and what is Alice's responsibility?

Stage 3: What is the dilemma about?

Once we have gone through the previous stages and completed a thorough analysis, we can find out what the dilemma is – that is, the nature of the real problem. What is the question that is asked or that you ask yourself? Is there really a choice; is it a dilemma after all? Is it an ethical or a moral dilemma, in other words, is it 'human welfare' that is under discussion?

> Taking these considerations into account, we could come to the conclusion that in Alice's case it is not necessary to go into the dilemma between Alice and the team. First, other questions about Alice, the team and the organisation should come up for discussion. Other aspects may have to be considered first and thus get priority.

Stage 4: What are the alternatives?

This is the crucial stage of the process. Creativity is vitally important. Before you can form an opinion or take a decision, it is important to consider your options. Sometimes you can come up with a compromise or a counter-proposal. In some cases, this helps to broaden your options. When listing the alternatives, the advantages and disadvantages, consequences, feasibility and the price to pay are mapped out. Finally, the link with values and interests is made. In other words, to whose responsibility will we appeal? To carry out this stage optimally, students will have to be encouraged to work freely in a critically creative manner. Often I encourage the students literally to get out of their normal discussion pattern, because I notice that set habits in meetings may lead to rigidity and can block creativity. So the task for this stage might comprise:

> To find creative solutions for Alice's situation, send discussion groups out for a walk or ask them to lie on the floor or stand on their heads to analyse the case literally from all perspectives. No alternative should be rejected, and the advantages and disadvantages of every option should be listed.

Stage 5: What is the conclusion?

At this stage, the alternatives are being weighed against each other. Based on the listed facts and the priorities set in terms of values and interests, alternatives are compared with each other and the advantages and disadvantages are balanced against each other. After that, a choice is made. At first, an idea has to be formed of the different values and standards in the case concerned. Further, we need to check whether there is a conflict of values/standards and what hierarchical system of ordering the values/standards can be employed. What decision do we take and which arguments do we use to justify ourselves? In order to reach this decision we can ask ourselves the following questions: Are standards/regulations absolute? Whose responsibility is the most decisive?

> Applied to Alice, on the one hand, a whole debate on the team's agreements and on the purpose of these agreements could develop. On the other hand, a process could be started in which Alice herself remains the owner of 'her problem' and in which she is guided in her quest for an answer.

Stage 6: How to carry out the decision?

Finally, it is time to act. The decision has to be executed. When it is your dilemma, you are the one that has to take the plunge and that has to carry out the decisions. When several people have taken the decision, it has to be decided who will carry out the decision.

The 'when' and the 'where' are always important, as it is also essential to handle ethical issues with care. Sometimes it takes courage do what, in your view, needs to be done. An important question here is: what agreements have to be made to follow up the case? For example, we might ask:

> Does George have to take up the situation with Alice, or is the whole team involved, and can this situation give rise to a group discussion?

Stage 7: Evaluation and reflection

The aim of this stage is quite different from the other stages in the staged plan. In the final assessment, a number of meta-questions are asked about how the staged plan has been completed and about the quality of the discussion. We take stock of how we have completed the plan and we ask ourselves the following questions:

> In addition to the assessment of the problem and the decisions, we will also need to have an eye for the process between those involved in the staged plan.

The importance of communication

Working with the ethical issues that present themselves in practice means organising good communication within an organisation. Good communication implies that the conversation happens efficiently and that it is problem-oriented and problem-solving. However, good communication is more than simply exchanging information or using efficient conversation techniques. Apart from the content and the efficiency of the message, good communication requires an ethical relationship between people. Both conversation partners have to be willing to take seriously each other's questions, protests, frustrations and unspoken expectations. This is not the same as complying with someone else's wishes. Without sincerity, the conversation becomes streamlined in advance, and it is not about real human communication, but about a good strategy to achieve something, a form of seduction, control or blackmail.

Communication as a strategy or technique is radically different from communication as an ethical relationship. The latter requires a very demanding relationship of mutual respect and responsibility, which is not always the case for communication strategies such as marketing, advertising, demagogy or image-building.

To be able to make an ethical judgement, a reference point or standard is required. A reasonable standard would be that morally good communication aims at consulting all the groups involved, especially the weakest partners. It should be a fair communication with all groups involved, even with those sometimes forgotten or neglected. It is obvious that we cannot make the judgement from some kind of detailed normative ethics, like a Christian or ideological attitude to life, but from communicative ethics, in which the quality of the communication process is emphasised. Communicative ethics emphasises dialogue in a pluralist context, while normative ethics pays special attention to the development of a fundamental conviction.

The quality of the communication between the partners is connected to a number of conditions that must be fulfilled as a necessary condition:

- the willingness to have open communication;
- clear agreements on the areas of responsibility and the power of decision-making;
- attempts to solve controversies and the right to have dissident opinions.

Only if groups pay attention to these preconditions can the results of a staged plan be considered satisfactory – not in the sense of an 'ideal' solution or a 'general conclusion', but rather as having a good feeling about the discussion and as having reached an interim result that can be worked with.

Conclusions

A staged plan is a very useful tool for helping to structure discussions on ethical topics and giving participants the possibility to make observations from a distance and explore a range of alternatives. However, it is not a miracle-worker, and the main condition of its use is ethical communication. It is important, therefore, that students also learn some discussion techniques (for example, practising Socratic dialogue as outlined in Chapter 5 would be a useful exercise). As with Socratic dialogue, working with the plan requires a strong commitment from the student group. Indeed, students sometimes complain that it takes a lot of time to use the staged plan. Furthermore, by using this step-by-step method, the discussion can become very personal and participants can be pulled into very interrogating confrontations with their own values and attitudes. Teachers or facilitators need to be aware of the conditions necessary for an effective debate, and participants must have the opportunity to indicate their limits and withdraw from the discussion if necessary.

7.

An ethical decision-making model

Jochen Windheuser

Introduction

This chapter takes as its starting point the nature of the work of the social professions as involving problem-solving in complex situations. The ideas of Dietrich Dörner (a German psychologist) on balanced decision-making are explored in the context of a complex case study, using role play, with a group of students.

A problem-solving approach in social work

As Miller, Galanter and Pribram (1960) point out, the general problem-solving model is constitutive of human thinking and acting. Thus it is not surprising that professional acting in social work is described again and again in terms of this model (see Franke and Sander-Franke, 1998, as one elaborated example, and chapter 6 in this book). Siegel (1984, p. 328) compared the general problem-solving process, the research process and the process of intervention in social work in an interesting synopsis. The steps of the basic model are typically specified as:

- analysing the problem;
- defining the goal;
- planning (including searching and evaluating the alternatives);
- decision making;
- realising;
- controlling the success.

Of course, the terms 'problem' and 'problem-solving' do not have a single definition. To be helpful, they should be defined narrowly. It can be useful in professional situations to differentiate between 'tasks' and 'problems' (Possehl, 1993). A task involves acting routinely, whereas solving problems requires a more conscious and creative process. The latter is usually the case when the situation is new, surprising and/or unexpected (typically when disturbances or failures happen), and with increasing complexity of the situation.

The 'complexity' of social work problems

A subject perceives a situation as complex, when there exist several alternative courses of action and/or external or internal (cognitive, emotional, ethical) conflicts. Objectively a situation may be described as complex the more it is:

- hard to survey – the situation includes more information than the subject can actually handle;
- built as a network – the elements and states of the situation or system are multiply- related to each other;
- internally dynamic – things change independently with time, even if the decision-maker does not intervene;
- opaque – some information, which may be important for the decision, is not available or unclear,
- unstable – all prognoses are based only on probability and plausibility and therefore not at all certain (for more details, see Reither, 1997).

In practical social work, everyday problems fall into most of these categories. The professional has (or may have, if he/she wants to) a great deal of information, but most of it is unclear and limited. The people and institutions involved in a life situation are on different levels in relation to each other and form an inter-connected network, which is always developing in an independent and often unpredictable manner.

Take, for example, a conference organising the helping process for a child in a children's residential care home. Around the table, there may be sitting: the child, representatives of the child and youth welfare office, youth workers and/or educators on the staff of the home, parents, a paediatrician, teachers, and so on. In addition, 'virtually' in the background there may be: grand parents, playmates, neighbours, the management of the home, and so on. They give plenty of information, but are often not willing or motivated to give it very clearly and fully. They may all know each other from a long history which the social worker perhaps does not share, and they are related by hidden prejudices and mental reservations, which change constantly under the influence of diverse factors from outside or from the system itself.

Finding a balanced decision in a complex situation – a value?

The social worker's task now is to make sure that every decision he or she takes keeps the whole system of people involved in balance. It is a matter for discussion whether this is a value in itself. It may be argued that any aspect of the rationality of a decision or an act is ethically neutral. Following this argument, correct conclusions, complete analyses, considering lateral consequences, as well as finding a balance between different arguments, may be aspects of methodological quality and thus *professional standards* or *tools* which help to decide better between values, rather than *ethical values* in themselves.

However, I think this view is too narrow. Of course, values have to be formulated as aspects of factors other than the social worker him or herself – for example, as aspects of the client (especially his or her emancipation or autonomy) or aspects of a group or the society. But there are professional standards in social work that are closely related to such values. 'Do not act instead of the client' is in this sense the methodological side of the value 'autonomy'; 'strengthen the weaker side' is the expression of 'emancipation' in methodological terms. These methodological aspects cannot be neutral in relation to the connected values. In a similar way, 'balanced decision-making' can be considered as strongly related to values like 'justice' or 'participation of all'. It cannot be considered as neutral – as if unbalanced decisions could be equally either just or unjust. Following only one or two 'good principles' may sometimes do more harm than good in professional situations, and a balanced decision may be the *only* ethically acceptable one. Therefore it is important to train the students by means of case studies, which challenge their balance-finding capacity.

Training students through using case studies has a long tradition in education of social workers. But it must be emphasised that teachers should not forget to educate students to work in unclear and complex situations; to find balanced decisions in this complexity; and to look at this task as an ethical one. Before exemplifying this, I will briefly discuss a cognitive-psychological approach to the analysis and development of decision-making capacities in complex situations.

A theoretical framework: the approach of Dietrich Dörner

Dietrich Dörner, a German psychologist, developed a decision-making framework which helped surmount a certain fixation in the psychology of thinking on convergent problem-solving. In the 1980s he created a special research design to investigate the creative decision-making behaviour in complex situations (Dörner, 1992, 1996; Dörner and Wearing, 1995).

The basic ideas of Dörner's approach

According to Dörner, the legacy of human evolution is what he calls a 'trouble-shooter' intelligence. Concerns used to be about supplies for the next winter, traps for wild animals or fights against a new group of strangers. All those problems only had an *ad hoc* importance; they occurred and had to be solved in a short-term manner. Modern life is different. Countless problems in a network, even worldwide, create long-term effects. They overtax our minds, because they seem to be insufficiently developed to deal with problems in such networks – and therefore training is needed. In order to demonstrate this restriction of the human mind, Dörner and his staff found a humorous example:

> The pool in the garden stinks! So: catching and storing the fishes, draining off the water. The bottom stinks, too! So: digging out and

taking away the mud. New gravel on the bottom, refilling with water, putting the water plants in again and the fishes. Result: one day of hard work and two dead fishes. The pool does not stink any more! Two months later: The pool in the garden stinks! ... (Dörner, 1992, p. 107)

Which professional does not know of analogous situations in social work? Of course, Dörner's invented gardener disregarded the character of the pool as a system comprising several components, with positive and negative feedback between them. Only a holistic view of the components and their reciprocal effects could lead to a solution.

Dörner draws attention to historical decisions with tremendous consequences where reciprocal effects were neglected in a similar manner, such as the construction of the Assuan dam in Egypt, which created a lot of important but insufficiently considered problems, mainly in agriculture.

In order to investigate such phenomena, Dörner invented a laboratory method, the computer simulation of complex situations (see Dörner et al., 1994). He put his experimental subjects in the role of a member of the Voluntary Overseas Service (a project called 'Tanaland') or of a mayor vested with far-reaching powers (project 'Lohhausen'). At several self-chosen points of decision-making, they could manipulate a number of variables. For example, they could sink a well or take actions against infant mortality in Tanaland; or promote investment or the construction of swimming baths in Lohhausen. The computer calculated the development of Tanaland or Lohhausen town up to the next chosen point of time and indicated to the experimental subjects the actual state it would be in according to a large number of criteria. Experts in development aid, agriculture, economics and so on had written the algorithms for these calculations.

Dörner completed this research by analysing well-documented historical misjudgements like the catastrophe at the Chernobyl (Czernobyl) nuclear power plant in Russia. The aim of his research was both to identify typical deficiencies in strategies of thinking, and also to find ways to prevent such mistakes by adequate training.

Typical deficiencies in strategies of thinking

Dörner elaborated a lot of typical deficient thinking strategies (Dörner 1992; Dörner and Schaub, 1994), including the following:

1) Insufficient analysis of the situation – This refers to the attitude: 'What is going wrong? We have to do something immediately against it!' Confronted with an increase in unemployment among young people, a 'bad' mayor reacts emotionally and, for example, puts pressure on the industry in town. Whereas a 'good' mayor initiates a data survey in order to start from secure facts.

2) Neglect of causal networks and of distant and collateral effects – It is typical to overlook negative feedback. The lines of reasoning often do not go far enough. Thus sinking wells in new pasturelands in order to increase the export of cattle ignores the reduction in ground water in Tanaland. One 'mayor', whose priority was to increase the happiness of the inhabitants, was surprised at lots of new people moving to Lohhausen (and thus neutralising some of his actions).

3) No attention is paid to the time span of a process – Typical here is the neglect of buffer and reinforcement effects. We have difficulties, for example, with situations in which anti-cyclic behaviour would be necessary, as is often the case with budgets (this is relevant in Lohhausen). A special source of mistakes is our notorious underestimation of exponential growth over time (for example, in the case of infection with HIV).

4) Methodological rituals – Experimental subjects tend to repeat measures only because they (for the present) do not show any negative effect – they behave ritually. For example, some super-mayors from time to time ritually increased the salaries in the watch factory at Lohhausen.

5) 'Projectism', 'ad-hoc-ism', the 'ballistic approach' – These strategies are especially in vogue, and Dörner describes them humorously. One over-taxed mayor gets the information that the pensioners of the town feel lonely, and in the time that follows he invests his energy completely into a project to set up more public call centres ('projectism'). 'Ad-hoc-ism' means: I am involved in action A, and when receiving certain information I jump out of action A and start with a completely different action. Finally, a 'ballistic' mayor sees the problem and shoots at random – thinking perhaps it can be solved in this way. For example, sales of watches made in Lohhausen are down, so let us try with a new design!

Characteristics of 'good decision-makers'

In his Lohhausen project, Dörner additionally put the question the other way around: What are the characteristics of 'good decision-makers'? Are there any systematic differences in behaviour between successful and less successful experimental subjects?

1) Collecting data – When looking for information, successful 'mayors' more often follow 'why?'questions compared with unsuccessful colleagues. They also more frequently seek special information in order to prove their hypotheses.

2) Communication – Good decision-makers spend more time organising their own work, especially by 'thinking out loud' and thus sharing their thoughts with others. They also give (virtual) co-workers more responsibility.

3) Number of decisions – Good decision-makers tend to take more decisions and learn to make more complex decisions. On the average, they begin with eight decisions per occasion (a time stop in the computer program) compared with six decisions made by the bad decision-makers; they rise to 18 decisions per occasion compared to eight of the poorer group. Another aspect of this behaviour is that they take more decisions in the context of a single intention, which can also be interpreted as a sign of thinking in networks.

4) Stability of deciding – Successful mayors are more stable in their decision-making process. That means, they show less tendency to change the themes of their decisions from one occasion to the next, thus keeping the spectrum of decisions more constant. And, of course, they are less inclined to change the direction of their decisions radically.

It is worth noting that one group of experimental subjects comprised professional managers, and they had the best average performance as 'mayors' – perhaps because they were more familiar with decision-making in complex situations.

Training to prevent such mistakes
In conjunction with this research, Dörner and his co-workers developed training methods and applied them especially in the economic field (Reither, 1997). At the core of these methods is interactive computer programs which simulate complicated, networked and self-dynamic model situations, and styles and strategies of decision-making are individually analysed and trained.

Considering the various possible aims of these training programmes, the personal ability to create a well-balanced process of decision-making is the most interesting in our context. The immediate feedback provided by the computing process seems to be crucial for effective learning.

Transfer of the approach into ethical training

The idea of transferring this approach to the education of social workers in professional ethics is based on the conviction that ethical behaviour in professional social work has to be expressed in the whole context of a case or problem process, not only in answering single questions posed by situations. Cases and social problems can be simulated by role plays (rather than by computers). Role playing case stories in several steps is a traditional method in social work education. To adapt this method to the task discussed here means: writing realistically complex cases, which include ethical problems and dilemmas, and writing a kind of script, which describes possible developments, depending on which decisions are made by the protagonist.

A case story

The following case story, the essentials of which are reported by a social worker from a Caritas advice centre for homeless people (Zentrale Beratungsstelle Osnabrück, 1999), may serve as an example:

> *A case of arrest and a network of trust* – After a client lost his job and accommodation, he lived for nearly two years without money on the street. For six months he was under the supervision of the Caritas advice centre for homeless people and lived in the meantime in a transitional home (that is, in accommodation provided by the centre in order to train people in living independently again – with the aim of finding 'normal' accommodation later). Within this period, the employment office obtained vocational retraining for him. This retraining, including an in-house placement of six months, fitted his acquired trade and offered him essential new skills, thus increasing his chance of being reintegrated into the job market. The client got 560 Euros in reduced unemployment benefit per month for all his expenditure including the rent for his accommodation. In the continuous supervision by the centre, the high motivation of the client to continue the retraining and a strong mutual trust between the client and the social worker were noticed.
>
> About four weeks after the beginning of the retraining, the police delivered the client a warrant for his arrest. This arrest for 22 days was to extort from the client the payment of 550 Euros because of an administrative offence (although, obviously, the arrest would not pay off the fine). After being informed by the centre about the client's situation, the police allowed some time to work with his problems. Within this time, one week later, the police came up with another warrant for his arrest, this time for 40 days on another charge, because he did not pay a second fine. On this charge, another prosecutor has jurisdiction. The police trust the social workers in the advice centre a lot, because they have had good contact over years and know they are reliable. However, this is not the case in relation to the prosecutors' offices. Of course, neither the employment office nor any other governmental office gives money for fines. The Caritas centre may be more flexible, but the budgets in social care are very restricted nowadays ...

Working with social work students on this case (in the context of a psychological seminar about thinking, rather than teaching ethics), I not only invited them to find in their discussion 'good', 'balanced' solutions, but also 'bad' solutions, which are bad because they are influenced by deficient strategies of thinking, that is, stressing only *one* positively valued ethical aspect, neglecting distant and/or collateral effects. Here are some examples of those 'bad' solutions the students found:

- *The client should be put under arrest, because he is responsible for his own faults and has to pay for them. This is the only way for him to learn.* The students commented that, of course, this 'solution' overemphasizes one single ethical argument and neglects a lot of obvious negative consequences: his self-confidence and his motivation are endangered, he will be disappointed about the social worker and the centre, the employment office may be very cautious about arranging a second vocational retraining for him, and so on. And the fine still remains unpaid!
- *The social worker lends the fines (altogether nearly 1000 Euros) – privately, or out of the 'petty cash' of the centre. The client discharges it during his retraining by small instalments, and later eventually more.* The students' comments were that this is a typical naïve helping perspective, possibly highly valued but unprofessional. The risk the social worker runs cannot be calculated (for example, getting in conflict with his employer), and it even endangers the trusting relationship between the client and worker. It underestimates the autonomy of the client. And what will the social worker do if other clients hear what happens and demand similar support?
- *Through the good relationship with the police, the social worker obtains a commitment that the prosecutors' offices will allow some more delay. Within this time span, the client could try to earn money and pay the fine.* But students saw that a mere delay just puts the risk to one side. On the other hand, possible solutions which provided a *quick* and reliable payment of the fines always include problematic consequences: interruption of the retraining or even taking job in the 'informal economy' in addition, which is illegal and much too risky for the client (and even for the social worker, if he knows about or supports it).

The students then formulated a 'balanced' solution. This entailed the following plan:

> Because of the trusting relationship between social worker and client, and the client's high motivation, the social worker should try to ensure that the courts allow time for payment by instalments which do not endanger the client's retraining process. In order to convince the courts to accept these guarantees, the social worker should ask the police to confirm that the advice centre has proved to be very reliable over years. On the other hand, the client would have to agree that the social worker would get the right to manage his bank account over a certain period of time to ensure the instalments are paid.

According to the reasoning given by the students, each side contributes to the solution by taking (controllable) risks, but also benefits from it, and no special ethical principles or boundaries are violated.

In a first round of role plays, the student taking the role of the social worker tried to realise the parts of the plan. Other roles included: the 'prosecutor' who should be very rigid and a colleague of the social worker arguing for being more restrictive, boasting of collegial solidarity. The student playing the role of the social worker had to find his/her way through the resulting ethical demands and at the same time remain flexible.

Conclusions

This approach to learning develops students' awareness of the complexities of making decisions. It encourages them to explore all possible consequences of a decision, and to realise the dangers of coming to hasty or narrowly conceived solutions. By considering 'bad' as well as 'good' solutions, they are encouraged to see problems in a broad context. As with the 'seven steps' method outlined in Chapter 6, this model focuses attention on logic, argument and strategic planning, emphasising the rational aspects of decision-making. However, the addition of role play to explore the implementation of proposed solutions not only gives students the chance to test out the practicality of their plans, but also to feel what it might be like to be an actor in the case. Through the role play they may get in touch with feelings of anxiety, anger, sympathy or frustration, for example.

The ideas explored in this chapter should be seen as a stimulus, brought into the discussion about teaching ethics from an external point of view (psychology). This approach is, however, a very typical way to compose teaching programmes in social work education: professional social workers and practitioners, as well as colleagues from different disciplines, contribute to preparing the students for their task – to help people find a human and ethically responsible path through their often difficult and painful life situations.

8.

Exploring aspects of ethical theory through drama

Robert Langen

Introduction

This chapter presents a proposal about how to change teacher-centred teaching about theoretical approaches to ethics into student-centred learning. This is based on the use of a system for groups known as *Themenzentriertes Theater* (TZT) developed by Werthmüller (1993). Using the Kantian approach to ethics as an example, I explain the methodology of the TZT system in relation to one of the key themes in Kantian ethics, namely: 'respect for persons'. A selection of six sets of group exercises is offered, which invite the student group to tackle this theme in an active manner. I explain the function of the exercises and briefly discuss the implications of working with TZT for the roles of students and teachers.

Background

Students training for the social professions often find it hard to use particular ethical theories and approaches (such as, Kantian, utilitarian or virtue ethics, as presented in the literature of moral philosophy) in their practice. These theories appear to students to be written for an academic debate, which has little relevance for the ethical problems they have to solve in their everyday professional life. Therefore it is hard for teachers to bring together the world of moral philosophy and the concrete questions raised by future workers in social professions. There is obviously a requirement for didactic and methodological approaches that can mediate between aspects of ethical theory and the needs and learning conditions of students.

In 1976 the Swiss theatre director and psychologist Heinrich Werthmüller (1993) created the *Themenzentriertes Theater* (TZT), a learning and teaching method for groups in the tradition of humanistic psychology and pedagogy. Translated literally, *Themenzentriertes Theater* means 'theme-focused theatre'. This method aims to involve the cognitive, emotional and physical aspects of learning. According to Werthmüller, it is important that the whole human being participates in learning processes, with all its capacities. Learning must have an important meaning for the individual and the group. Its relevance must be produced by a defined connection between the specific subject matter, the group and its individual members. Using the Kantian approach to ethics as example of a subject matter, I will show how students can learn about aspects of an ethical theory through using the acting-orientated teaching and learning system of TZT. In order to do this I will present a flexible set of teaching and learning exercises for a group of 20 students.

The potential for use of TZT in teaching and learning about Kantian ethics

In explaining how we might use the TZT approach in relation to Kantian ethics, I will first briefly summarise the nature of Kantian ethics, and then explain the two key concepts that are fundamental to TZT ('subject matter' and 'immanent themes').

Kantian ethics – As outlined in the Appendix to Chapter 1, Kantian ethics is a system of ethics developed by the eighteenth-century German philosopher, Immanuel Kant, based on the fundamental principle of 'respect for persons'. Kant regarded this as a categorical imperative (a command that must be obeyed). According to Kantian philosophy, a 'person' is a being who is capable of rational thought and self-determined action, where 'rational' means the ability to give reasons for actions; and 'self-determining' entails acting according to one's own choices and desires and having the ability to make decisions. 'Respect' can be regarded as an 'active sympathy' towards another human being.

Subject matter – this is the material the group is going to work with, that is, the specific content, problem or phenomenon a group wants to learn about. It can be all kind of things, which may have a certain meaning for a group. For a class of students wanting to learn something about ethical theory, the Kantian approach could be the subject matter. But without any further preparation this approach will probably remain 'dead', meaningless and isolated from the professional and private life experiences of students. It may even have the effect of scaring students without a philosophical background, creating resistance before the learning process has started. A link between this anonymous subject matter and the students must be established. In the TZT-System this link is termed the 'theme immanent to the subject matter'.

Immanent themes – these are bridges between the subject matter and the learning group. They take important aspects of the subject matter and connect them with the interests and experiences of a group. As stated above, 'respect for persons', for example, is a crucial principle of the Kantian approach with a big influence on social professions (Banks, 2001, pp. 24-30). But what does unconditional 'respect for persons' mean in everyday professional life? What about practical experiences concerning what it means if this principle is maintained? How is the term 'respect' related to fear, acknowledgement, admiration, love or dignity? What has 'respect' got to do with nearness and distance in relationship to service users?

The incomplete collection of questions listed above highlights the variety of topics which are on the one hand inherent to 'respect for persons' and on the other hand close to different experiences of students in their private and professional contexts. In order entirely to bridge the gap between the subject matter and the learners the immanent themes are formulated in a way that provides an opportunity to act and involves the other members in the group. For example, we might choose the following statement in relation to Kantian ethics:

Together we'll find out what it means to pay/not to pay and to receive/not to receive respect.

Other immanent themes of the Kantian approach could deal with the categorical imperative: 'Your actions and my actions become law for everybody any time! What ways of acting are possible/impossible now?' or the Kantian conception of a person: 'What shall we do with people who are not able to determine their own actions?'

Using TZT in class: some examples

In order to facilitate an active exchange between students and the acquisition of experiences, the theme can be explored using exercises based on six different elements or dimensions that can be freely combined in the course of a lesson or a module. All these exercises are focused on the immanent theme.

1. ENTRANCE

If we imagine that our class of 20 students has just entered the classroom. They want to start working but they are still 'mentally absent' and are not in touch with the subject matter yet. The following exercise could promote their introduction to the content of the learning and the learning environment:

Entrance: Exercise 1
Instructions for students:
Move all over the room. When you meet one of your colleagues, show respect to him or her by offering an appropriate greeting and other signs or salutes.

Purpose/aim: Students can realize the active part of paying respect and the feeling of being treated respectfully. They can also contact their colleagues at the beginning of their cooperation in a positive way.

Using this exercise as a kind of warm-up provides a secure and gentle acquaintance with the subject matter, the immanent theme and the other members of the group. It considers the fact that human beings often feel uneasy in new situations, expecting unknown challenges. A new subject matter, a new topic, which perhaps has to be tackled with a new team needs an atmosphere which invites participants to approach it gradually, without pressure to expose themselves, or fear of difficult tasks.

In my example, the ritual of greeting, which is a very well known way of showing respect and acknowledgement, is at the centre of attention. The group is offered the opportunity to feel and comprehend a deeper sense of greeting: to pay positive attention to another person or to show a minimum of acceptance. It is useful also to make the opposite experience available with another exercise:

Entrance: Exercise 2
Instructions for students:
Move all over the room, but avoid any kind of contact.

Purpose/aim: Students can realize how even in a 'laboratory' situation, the atmosphere cools down if minimal signs of paying respect are absent.

Since the learning culture in schools and universities often focuses on cognition, students may feel alienated when they are asked to 'walk around and greet one another'. Therefore it might be helpful if they are given an additional task to observe themselves and the reaction of the group and to exchange their observations afterwards. They might be asked to consider questions such as: 'How do I perform rituals of greetings?'; 'What are the reactions?'; 'What is the difference between the first and the second exercise in relation to atmosphere?'. This way even academically-trained people may understand that such exercises may better clarify the peculiarity of paying respect than just talking about it.

Nevertheless, it is important to respect the abilities of the group. If students with a low affinity to 'performing' are confronted with a task they perceive as an imposition, permanent resistance may deeply disturb the whole learning process. On the other hand, students who enjoy performing and who are familiar with experimental settings may ask for more demanding task. A further exercise might be as follows:

Entrance: Exercise 3

Instructions for students:
Split up in two groups: nobles and servants. The servants demonstrate how to pay respect to the nobles. After two minutes roles change.

Purpose/Aim: Students can realize that respect also has something to do with distance and submission.

'Entrance' exercises are comparatively simple to perform, involve the whole group at the same time (to prevent a high degree of exposure), get the group moving (to reduce inhibitions) and offer an introduction to the subject matter and immanent theme. Beyond that, they demonstrate the experience of the group with performing and experimental settings in order to offer tasks that fit the abilities of group members. The didactic intention must be clear and easy to understand.

2. FORMING SMALL GROUPS

The second element or dimension around which group exercises can be built is the formation of small groups. A group of 20 people working together as a whole is often too big for the different tasks the students have to deal with in the course of teaching. Therefore the class often needs to be split up in small groups. Even this 'organizational operation' can be implemented in a way that takes account of the needs of the group and specific aspects of subject matter and immanent theme:

Forming small groups: Exercise 1

Instructions for students:
Please line up by height. Then the tallest and the shortest person go together, until a group of four people has formed. After that the next tallest and shortest people come together until the whole class is divided into small groups of four.

Purposes/aims: The division of the class into small groups. Students become aware of height as a crucial factor in creating 'respect' according to at least a common understanding of the word.

The forming of (smaller) groups in teaching and learning situations deserves a lot of attention. Since we choose carefully in our private life the people we cooperate with in different contexts, it is also important to think about the criteria for deciding about who should work together in the classroom. TZT offers five different ways of forming groups, depending on the task to be done, the state of relationships in the whole class, the impact of the present situation and the number of members a small group should have.

The example above is an 'objective' way of forming a group with four people. By 'objective' I mean that the criterion for composing the group (height) is 'defined from outside'. So the members of the class do not get burdened with the responsibility of deciding about how to compose the group and they are released from the fear of not being chosen. The link to the immanent theme is represented by height, which in the spirit of common sense often is associated with 'respect'.

The next exercise belongs to what might be called the 'comparing and completing' method of forming groups:

Forming small groups: Exercise 2

Instructions for students:
Each student should choose spontaneously one category of people who especially deserve respect – for example, 'older people' or 'police officers'. Note the name of your category of people in big letters on a piece of paper. Walk around and show it to the others. Form a small group of four students by combining four of the categories of people together. The criterion for forming your groups should be to consider what the categories of people listed on your pieces of paper have in common.

Purposes/aims: The whole class is divided into four-person groups. Students can take over responsibility for group formation by using facts/arguments and considering personal sympathies.

This second example considers that, as a matter of fact, group formation is inevitably linked with choice. We all tend to choose people for our activities who have our sympathy. By this behaviour we run the risk of missing important experiences of cooperation with people who do not belong to our first preference. The 'comparing and completing' way of forming groups encourages students to consider objective facts in combination with personal affection.

As I already explained, 'objective' ways of forming small groups are useful if students are not to be burdened with the problem of choice and the embarrassing experience of not being chosen. Since the composition of objectively formed groups is not based on voluntary choice, students should stay together in these groups only for small exercises which will not take too much time. The 'comparing and completing' method is indicated when the group has already developed a basis of trust and the task to be solved is more complex and needs a more stable group.

The TZT system also provides the 'spontaneous' way of forming groups, which, for example, combines people who are just standing together. At the beginning of a lesson, students may be talking to each other or standing together in small groups. These formations can be taken spontaneously as small groups for well-structured and relatively short tasks so that the groups can soon split up again.

The 'imperative' way of forming small groups ('You and you and you go together!') is indicated when the teacher realises that for reasons of group dynamics, for instance, certain students should work together for a while.

Practising the 'subjective' variation, students decide themselves and by their own subjective criteria with whom they go together – or not. This is the most demanding way because both the whole responsibility for formation of groups and the risk of being faced with a refusal has to be taken by the individuals involved. Therefore the 'subjective' way should only be applied when groups already have a certain level of mutual trust, security and maturity to cope with refusals.

The comparatively large selection of methods of forming groups is designed to broaden the opportunity for students to have experiences with many different small group compositions. Beyond that it is an attempt to tackle consciously and openly the everyday themes: 'I would like to work with you, but I'm afraid to be rejected' or 'I do not want to work with you, but I don't like to turn you down' or 'You aren't one of the people I normally prefer, but I'll cooperate with you because it's reasonable'.

3. SITUATION

After the class is divided into small groups each comprising four students, a further element of TZT can be introduced, relating to the 'situation' or 'scenario'.

Situation: Exercise 1

Instructions for students (preparation time: 10 minutes; time to perform: 2 minutes):
Please prepare in your small groups the following scenario:
On Noah's ark two lions and two antelopes must share a cabin. They negotiate possibilities of coexistence.

Purpose/aim: Students can experience actively ways of showing and receiving respect from the perspective of the powerful and the powerless.

The situation is the centrepiece of the elements of TZT, and allows students to try out different possibilities of acting in the protected framework of role play and fiction. The basic structure for the situation's content (the instructions for the students) focuses again, like all elements of TZT – on the immanent theme (in this case, paying and receiving respect). In this exercise all animals on Noah's ark deserve an unconditional respect because they were all created equal by God. Neither lions nor antelopes can claim preferential treatment, they have to consider the situation of all individuals involved. The roles provide opportunities to pay respect by asking about needs, showing empathy, and accepting the peculiarities of the others. The feeling of safety linked with respect is very important too.

Whereas in this example of a scenario the substantial actions are related to paying respect, the next exercise focuses on the discussion about who deserves respect at all:

Situation: Exercise 2

Instructions for students (preparation time: 10 minutes; time to perform: 2 minutes):
Please prepare in your small group the following scenario:
Two punks and two older people enter a tram. There are only two seats left ...

Purpose/aim: Students can explain, discover, defend or challenge their own claims and those of others on the theme of 'respect'.

Situations are often based in the area of fiction to prevent a direct reproduction of occurrences in professional practice that can be judged as 'right' or 'wrong'. It is crucial that there is a certain tension maintained by a problem that calls for action. This problem is defined by opposite roles (such as lions and antelopes), a possible conflict (not enough seats) or an unexpected event. The role becomes the vehicle that provides the chance to try out new ways of acting without serious consequences in real life. For example, as a lion one can rehearse what it is like to empathise with the weaker antelope and show respect for it, although normally it would be regarded as an animal to be preyed upon. The old woman can practise claiming respect, while the punk can practise challenging it.

It is important to limit the preparation time (10 minutes at the maximum). Students should not be seduced into attempting to present a perfect 'theatre performance'. A 'situation' or 'scenario' is a short clip that shows action and reveals problems without an ending or a convenient solution. 'Situations' deliver materials for discussion, reflection and deliberation.

If, for example, a class of 20 students is divided up in five smaller groups of four people in each (see exercises on group formation), five different ways of performing a scenario will be presented for the four groups not playing at any one time. These groups, taking over the function of audience, can give feedback from the outside and start a discussion with the actors, asking, for example: 'How did the lions and antelopes cope with the situation?'; 'Were the lions able to show respect?'; 'What concepts of respect were presented in the discussion between punks and older people?'.

In this way a lot of contributions for discussion about 'respect' come together. Finally this discussion can be made fruitful for transfer into practice.

4. REALISATION

The challenge presented to students in the next TZT element, 'realisation', is of a completely different nature, as the exercise below shows:

Realisation: Exercise 1

Instructions for students (groups of four people; preparation time: 60 minutes):

Imagine 10 service users with different problems (addiction, disabilities, experiences with violence, racism, behavioural problems …). Try to order them according to the following criterion: which of these service users has good prospects, and which has only a slim chance of getting respect? Try to explain your decision for every service user by bringing in (if possible) your experiences and examples. Record your results and arguments on flipcharts for presentation in the plenary session.

Purpose/aim: Students can realise the relation between status of service users and their chances of gaining respect. They also realise conditions and attributes that influence status.

While the 'situation' operates in the area of fiction, 'realisation' works with reality. 'Realisation' tends to produce concrete results (for example, a list of the range of service users related to the prospect they may have of getting respect). This is shaped by discussions inside the small group and later on at the plenary session. 'Realisations' provide space for exchange of arguments, debate and information. The task of reading, in the role of an expert group, a text about the crucial points of the Kantian approach in order to explain the content to the other colleagues afterwards would be a classic realisation. Problems emerging from practice and appropriate coping strategies find their place in the structure of realisation too, as is demonstrated in the following exercise:

Realisation: Exercise 2

Instructions for students (groups of four people; preparation time: 60 minutes):

Remember situations you have experienced in your practice when, in your view, people were treated without respect. Describe the situation to the other members of your group. Try to find out reasons or circumstances promoting such kinds of occurrences. Work out alternative courses of action. Collect your proposals for sharing in a plenary session.

Purpose/aim: Students can critically reflect on professional practice and discuss/find out appropriate ways of acting.

The 'realisation' element of TZT focuses on intellectual needs of students and the analysis of the subject matter. It is the fact-related 'counterweight' to the 'situation' where the role of emotion and the relevance of a problem for the individual/ group is the particular focus of attention. Therefore 'realisations' should consist of concrete tasks closely related to professional reflections and practice problems. They also pass on information, explanations and exercises necessary to go on with the subject matter. 'Realisations' tend to be time consuming. They usually need stable small groups able to maintain work for a longer period.

5. IMPROVISATION

In addition to close contact with reality, students should encounter some experiences, attitudes and aspects that mainly emerge from themselves – the element of 'improvisation'.

Improvisation: Exercise 1
Instructions for students (group of four people; preparation time: 10 minutes):
Working together, create with your bodies a 'sculpture' with the title 'respect'. The audience (the groups not involved at any one time) should express loudly the associations they have when looking at this sculpture.

Purpose/aim: Students can express their personal imagination of 'respect' in body language. They can also realize the importance of body language as an impulse to pay or not to pay respect.

'Improvisation' uses fantasy and creativity as a powerful source for development. Instructions are very minimal (in this example, they are only given the terms 'sculpture' and 'respect') and it is left to the group what to do about it. There is no prescription for direction, there is no expectation about a certain result. The only condition is the focus on the immanent theme. The purpose of 'improvisation' is to extend the boundaries related to the immanent theme and subject matter. Here is a second example:

Improvisation: Exercise 2
Instructions for students (group of four people; preparation time: 10 minutes):

Create a scene where the following sentence is shouted: 'What irreverent behaviour!'

Purpose/aim: Students can approach the 'respect-phenomenon' by a negative example serving as basis for a discussion about conceptions of 'respect'.

Improvisations tend to open new perspectives about a subject matter or an immanent theme. The intention of this element of TZT is to challenge. The group has to exchange and to negotiate about a small impulse and must find a way to express the emerging ideas in a communicative way. They need to discuss where a scene dealing with irreverent behaviour could happen: in a classroom, a church or the summit of Mount Everest, for example? They may consider what body language reveals about our imagination and attitudes relating to respect, and how deep its impact is on our behaviour. The 'snowball effect' of improvisations is very welcome: Associations provoked by acting out the impulses towards improvisation may, for example, become the basis of new realisations. At least they are perceptions able to influence the further thinking and feeling of students.

6. EXIT

With the next exercise, students can be led out of a demanding working day. The exercise is to be performed by the whole class again at the same time:

Exit: Exercise 1
Instructions for students (all students):
Line up in two rows facing each other. State loudly in one sentence the most important outcomes of this day (lesson) for you. Look at each other's faces, bow to each other and drift slowly apart …

Purpose/aim: Students can gather together the most important results of their work and bring the work with the subject matter and the cooperation with their colleagues to a preliminary close without an abrupt breaking off.

Another variation is as follows:

Exit: Exercise 2

Instructions for students (all students):
Come together in a circle. Tell the group, if you wish, about your most important experiences today. After that, say 'goodbye' (only with your eyes), slowly make a 180° turn, stay for one more moment in the circle (with faces pointed outside now), then leave the circle slowly …

Just as the first element of TZT, 'entrance', provides a first contact between individuals, the group, subject matter and immanent theme, the last element, 'exit', offers an opportunity to leave the subject and the people involved in an adequate way. 'Exits' are designed to summarize results (as in the examples above), order facts, define problems which could not be solved yet and prepare materials for the next working session. They also provide a time and structure in which to say 'good bye' to colleagues. In other words, the element of TZT called 'exit' tries to end temporary work and relationships in a gentle way in order to make the change into another context possible. In my examples, saying 'goodbye' is realised by nearness (students standing in two lines close by or in a circle), which slowly turns to distance.

Implications of working with TZT

TZT should not be regarded merely as a collection of themes and exercises to be applied whenever there is some free time. Working with TZT entails aiming at fundamental changes of priorities and roles in the classroom. Students become active learners, bringing in their very personal experiences and biographies and taking over more responsibility for the creative shaping of their learning. The purpose of learning through TZT is not an accumulation of knowledge as an end in itself, but the acquisition of skills, expertise and the ability to act professionally.

Teachers change from being transformers of knowledge, to take on a role as moderators of the learning process. They accompany their students during this process, providing and maintaining the framework for learning experiences. This entails that:

- The teacher defines the subject matter and the immanent themes. Experienced groups should be involved in this task progressively;
- The teacher creates the exercises and combines them into learning units. Experienced groups should be involved here too;
- The teacher leads the plenary discussions and helps the group to organise the collection and recording of results;
- The teacher uses group dynamics as a driving force for learning processes and takes resistances as relevant contributions to communication, waiting for an appropriate answer. Therefore the teacher has to find out, for example, the 'theme of the group', which is, according to Werthmüller, the sum of all matters, attitudes and fantasies in relation to the immanent theme, including those of which individual members of the group are aware and unaware. These themes intertwine in the group and can be a support or a burden. If, for instance, a group has the theme: 'We are very curious and therefore happy about every learning offer and input presented by a teacher', then it will probably be easy to work with 'respect for persons'. If the attitude of the group is: 'We dislike all authorities', then it might be harder to offer lessons about 'respect for persons', as resistance is already present in the group. The role of 'punk' in 'Situation: Exercise 2' given earlier would perhaps be suitable to promote discussion about the resistance of people who 'dislike all authorities'.
- The teacher observes the development of the group to adjust the degree of responsibility for students and the level of the tasks.

Teachers and students who engage in learning through TZT get the chance to face fascinating learning experiences having a direct impact on professional action. Probably they are also confronted with their attitudes, emotions and the problematic sides of their personality and action.

Bearing this in mind, teachers may be anxious about whether TZT may provoke group dynamic forces with which they will be unable to cope.

However, whether this happens depends on the closeness of the subject matter to the group. For instance, if a group wants to learn something about its own dynamics, then the dynamics of this group form the subject matter of the work with TZT. All immanent themes and all exercises will focus on this group and its dynamics. This learning programme, which of course is very close to the group, should be moderated by a teacher with experience and expertise in working with group dynamics. But if the subject matter has a certain distance from the group, the dynamics will not be so difficult to handle. On the contrary, in this case group dynamics may become the most important energy source to develop learning.

Conclusions

Theoretical approaches to ethics probably constitute a subject matter that has a certain distance from students in the social professions. Conventional teacher-centred settings often face the problem that students without philosophical education find it hard to relate to this subject. The difficult language and the specific points of view which often cannot be comprehended by students give these approaches the status of an alien element which seems to have no relevance for professional practice. Here the TZT method could be a chance to highlight the impact of moral philosophy on ethical thinking in private and professional life. Furthermore, students have the opportunity to apply and challenge the conceptualising structures of theoretical approaches to ethics through their own actions. So teaching ethical theories through the use of TZT could become a chance to change abstract and marginalized knowledge into useful skills integrated into professional action. It encourages students to become active learners who progressively take over the responsibility for the creative shaping of their learning, while the teacher's role changes from that of a transformer of knowledge into a moderator of learning processes.

9.

Integrating the teaching of ethics into the curriculum

Helene Jacobson Pettersson

Introduction

This chapter discusses how the ethical awareness of students in the social professions can be developed by integrating the teaching of ethics into the curriculum throughout the whole of a study programme. It is based on the experiences of the social work programme at the University of Kalmar in Sweden. This chapter describes how ethics is taught and the issues that are emphasised, in relation to course content and sequence. Some of the implications for teachers and the benefits for student learning are discussed, particularly in relation to links between theory and practice.

Teaching ethics

The idea being implemented at Kalmar is that ethics should form a strand in the content of all courses during the three-and-a-half-year programme. The aim is to improve students' knowledge and awareness of ethics in social work in their training as part of a cumulative process. Although there are no specific courses in ethics, certain sessions are devoted to the subject. Reamer (1997, p. 169), a professor in the School of Social Work, Rhode Island College, USA, reports that: 'only a handful of social work education programs require students to take a full, discrete course on social work ethics'. He surmises that: 'Most students are in fact introduced to the subject in the context of required and elective courses'. According to Reamer, social workers in the past have not been very well prepared to deal with ethical dilemmas in practice. This is partly due to the fact that there has not been a critical mass of literature on ethics in social work until the last 25 years, and also that there has not been enough teaching in the subject in the formal education of social workers. Although Reamer appears to be critical of the fact that few social work education programmes have specific courses on ethics, he does find persuasive the pedagogical arguments for having the subject integrated into other courses spread throughout the educational programme. The arguments of the teaching staff at the University of Kalmar for choosing to integrate the teaching of ethics into different courses are mainly that the personal growth of students in ethical awareness is a process that takes time.

Teaching ethics is an example of how we work at the University of Kalmar to meet the key aims of the study programme in social work. The aims include the further development of the student's ability to meet people in an empathic manner with flexibility and openness, and heightening students' awareness of their own attitudes and values, as well as stimulating an analysis of these in their personal and professional development (Department of Health and Behavioural Sciences, 2000, p. 2). These are overall aims intended to influence all courses in the study programme. The system guiding higher education in Sweden is regulated by the Higher Education Act, 1992. In this Act there is no explicit mention of knowledge and awareness of ethics. By writing these aims in our local study programme we have ensured that the dimension of ethical awareness is given a place in the curriculum. Other countries have a national curriculum, such as USA, where the following mandate concerning the teaching of social work values and ethics has been prescribed since 1992 in the guidance for social work education programmes nationwide:

> Programs of social work education must provide specific knowledge about social work values and their ethical implications, and must provide opportunities for students to demonstrate their application in professional practice. Students must be assisted to develop an awareness of their personal values and to clarify conflicting values and ethical dilemmas. (Reamer 1997, p.170)

What Reamer formulates above is very much in accordance with how we look at our commitment to give an educational programme in social work at the University of Kalmar.

The social work programme at Kalmar

The social work programme at Kalmar takes three and a half years and leads to a Bachelor in Social Work, carrying 210 ECTS (European Credit Transfer Scheme). It has developed from á former Diploma in Social Care. The new programme started in September 2001 and to date we only have students in Years One and Two. The description of the courses and teaching that is given here is, therefore, based on our experiences so far, our plans for the rest of the programme and our experiences from former programmes.

The teaching, both in ethics and in other subjects, is based on a problem-oriented method of working. This takes the form of lectures, methods training, tutorials, seminars ánd field-related studies. Several of these pedagogical methods are used to encourage the students to develop the capacity for independent and critical judgement and the ability to solve problems independently in social work. When we focus on ethics in the teaching, we aim to prepare students for difficult decision-making in their practical fieldwork and in their future professional roles as well as for research.

Teaching ethics in basic theoretical courses and social welfare legislation

The first year of study is a theoretical introduction into the core subject, social work, complemented by subjects relevant to social work such as sociology, psychology, and social welfare legislation. The ethics strand is most explicit in the courses entitled 'Social Work' and 'Social Welfare Legislation – An Overview'.

The social work course

The aim of the course in social work is that the students should acquire not only a basic knowledge of the subject as an academic discipline but also as an applied field. Ethics is introduced to the new students by promoting the understanding of salient questions in the subject. Some of the recommended reading explicitly relates to ethics in social work. An introductory lecture in the subject is given. As social work is very much a value-based subject, the teaching in this phase is focused on discussing the relation between our view of life: what makes life worth living; our outlook on humanity; human dignity; people's capacity and resources to form their lives; our culture; and the influence of all these factors in forming our attitudes towards the people we meet and their needs. This forms the foundation from which we make our ethical reflections and decisions. In this context the concept of social pedagogical work is taken as an example of attitude in social work. The teaching could be described as being within the framework of what Blennberger (2000) understands ethics to be about, namely:

- The meaning of the principle of human dignity;
- The right actions and rules of behaviour;
- Good consequences and their allocation;
- Pleasant ethical personal qualities/moral maturity.

These areas are introduced in the teaching at a basic level and will be further developed later in the programme. The beginning of the programme is an appropriate time for students to discuss what the important topics are in a study programme to become a social worker. Reamer (1997) points out four such subjects:

1. *Values in social work.* Though there are some core social work values that seem to be valid for many countries, nevertheless conflicts exist. These conflicts might be between the values of the social worker and the client, or they might arise in the workplace between the values of the social worker and the employer. One more possibility for disagreement can be when the social worker has different values from the social profession itself as these are expressed, for example, in a professional code of ethics.
2. *Ethical dilemmas in practice.* Ethical dilemmas may arise at

different levels. There are ethical dilemmas linked to social policy and working in organisations. Practitioners face dilemmas also in relation to colleagues when it may be hard to choose where to place their loyalty, as well as in the encounter with the client when delivering services and support in relation to individuals, families or groups.

3. *Ethical-decision making skills.* Practitioners need to improve their knowledge of how to be able to do the right thing in different situations. This can be achieved by introducing different theoretical concepts of ethics to the students.

4. *Malpractice and ethical misconduct.* Today social workers are increasingly accused of malpractice and ethical misconduct. To avoid this it is necessary to know what constitutes malpractice and negligence. Social workers should also know about sexual abuse, breaking confidentiality, assumption of risk, malfeasance, and so on.

These areas are presented and discussed in the introduction to ethics. We inform the students that our ambition is to work with these questions during their education, in connection with relevant parts of the programme.

The students are asked to prepare themselves before the lecture by reading a chapter about ethics in social work written by Blennberger (2000). They are also given a task to reflect on and discuss certain key values and relate these to interventions in social work (see Appendix 9.1). The whole course is examined by a task that focuses on students' awareness of the meaning of social work. They have to relate the literature in social work to their pre-study concepts of social work and apply it to a given case of social problems (see Appendix 9.1 for details of this task). The subject or perspective of ethics is not explicitly asked for, but it is noticed if and how reference is made to the ethical dimensions by the way students handle the task.

The social welfare legislation course
The introductory course on social welfare legislation and civil rights enables the students to gain a basic understanding of law in a broad context. The aim is that students should understand

the system of legislation and its role in society. They should develop an understanding of their attitudes and of how they conduct themselves in relation to statutes and regulations. They analyse and discuss the meaning of key concepts such as 'democracy', 'right', 'duty', 'justice', 'welfare', 'equality', 'normality' and 'independence' and relate this to their understanding of the legislation in social welfare. The teaching is focused on the juridical aspect of the legislation: what it says and what the right thing to do is, according to the law. Then the students are asked to reflect on how this conforms with a good ethical solution. Do ethical considerations give an opportunity to interpret the law in another way? If that is the case, how could it be argued for? This is exemplified in one of the examinations for this course, where the students have to define the key concept 'custody' and describe the meaning and content of custody as it relates to children. They should also analyse and interpret the law to be able to declare what are the main reasons for deciding who is to have the custody of a child. The ethical dimension is not explicitly asked for in this exam either, but it is an integral part of the analysis, which would be incomplete without it.

Teaching ethics in further theoretical courses

The second year of study in social work is at a higher theoretical level. The course in social welfare work aims to improve students' knowledge of welfare politics and welfare work at various levels in Sweden and in the rest of Europe. In addition, the students are expected to acquire knowledge of social work in different operational areas with different target groups, as well as developing an increased understanding of the role of personal attitudes and values in social work. In this context students are given further theoretical teaching and tasks to encourage the development of their ethical knowledge and awareness. The core text by Henriksen and Vetlesen (2001) explores the field of ethics, describes the different theoretical approaches, and uses practical examples. Lectures are given on the subject of different perspectives on ethics, such as the ethics of duty, of discourse, of consequence, of virtue, and of care. The students are introduced to several definitions of 'ethics' and 'morals', along with the distinction between the three different types of ethical questions described by Banks (2001b, pp.10-11): ethical issues, ethical problems, and ethical dilemmas. The difference between primary/human and secondary/instrumental values is also discussed.

In the sessions on ethics we return to what was mentioned in the introductory lecture, namely: values in social work and ethical dilemmas in practice. We delve deeper into the discussion in dialogues with the students. 'Culture' is discussed as a significant key concept in connection with values in social work. Ethics is also discussed as a factor at different levels: the personal/individual, the institutional, and the structural. Since intercultural social work is a field that is permeated with ethical issues, it is useful to use it to illustrate ethics at these different levels. For example, racism, where it appears, affects intercultural communication. Dominelli (1997, p.7) defines three inter-related levels of racism – individual, institutional, and cultural – as follows:

- *Individual racism* is made up of attitudes and behaviour depicting a negative prejudgment of racial groups. Individual racist attitudes without institutional backing constitute racial prejudice.
- *Institutional racism* consists of customary routines which ration resources and power by excluding groups arbitrarily defined as racially inferior.
- *Cultural racism* is centred around those values, beliefs and ideas endorsing the superiority of white culture.

Racism is a complicated concept to discuss with the students. It is a political 'hot potato' and to some extent surrounded by taboo. However, using the word 'racism' rather than 'xenophobia' brings about a discussion of values and the meaning of ethics. If this discussion is conducted carefully, with space for reflection and in relation to ethics, it becomes a tool to clarify how these levels are interrelated. It also makes clear how handling questions from a low level of ethical awareness results in discrimination.

In the teaching programme the students are required to

reflect individually and in group discussions in order to explore their understanding of the concepts presented in the teaching and the literature. They work individually and in groups with case studies that are written by former students in fieldwork practice. Students also analyse and discuss cases that they have written themselves with the intention of training themselves to identify ethical questions and questions of values, to identify the individuals, groups and organisations involved, and to reflect upon optimal solutions.

Teaching ethics in courses integrating theory and fieldwork practice

Though the education is both vocationally-oriented and a preparation for postgraduate studies in social work, fieldwork practice is an important part of the students' education. Three concepts are important for both purposes of their education – 'values', 'knowledge' and 'skills'. These are interrelated and, as such, they become meaningful for integrating theory and practice. As already mentioned, social work is a value-based subject, which means values influence theoretical knowledge of social work, as well as the skills of the social workers. It is hard to give a precise answer to the question about how the learning process applies to the integration of theory and practice. Nevertheless, according to Thompson (2000), it is clear that 'person-centred' learning, in which people are encouraged to be responsible for their own learning and its practical application, is a requirement for the integration of theory and practice. The interrelation between values, knowledge and skills is implicit in Thompson's (2000) description of the relationship between theory and practice in the learning process. He suggests that the work of Kolb (1984) and other associated theorists has influenced very much the understanding of educational processes as an active process from reflected experience. Kolb illustrates the process in a learning cycle with four stages: concrete experience, reflective observation, abstract conceptualization, and active experimentation. According to Thompson (2000, p. 6), this perspective of integrating theory with practice and vice versa can be described as follows:

- Our experience has to be 'processed' (reflected upon, related to previous learning and applied to practice) in order for learning to take place. (Relate theory to practice)

- To make sense of our experience, we have to integrate it within a framework of pre-existing concepts: we have to make it part of our own theory base. (Relate practice to theory)

- Full learning only takes place when all the stages in Kolb´s learning cycle are reached. We might have acquired knowledge but we have not learnt until the knowledge is put into practice. Acquiring knowledge is only a part of the learning process. (Relate theory to practice)

- Learning is an active and self-directed process. Others can encourage our learning and the processes of relating theory to practice, but each of us has to take the responsibility of putting knowledge into practice and completing the learning cycle. (Relate theory to practice)

I will now describe the ethics teaching within the theory courses integrated with fieldwork practice in social work and will come back to these steps and link this to the idea of cumulative learning, mentioned at the beginning of this chapter. The experience at Kalmar of teaching theory partly integrated with the fieldwork practice suggests that by this means students have gained a good understanding and an improved knowledge of social work. The ambition is to encourage the students to integrate their experiences from fieldwork practice into the course at the university on the one hand, and, on the other hand, to stimulate them to reflect upon their practice through the filter of theoretical knowledge. Over the course of one year there will be theoretical courses integrated with two periods of fieldwork practice. During the first term the subject is 'Social Work and Method', and in the next term the subject is 'Social Welfare Legislation'.

The social work and method course
The social work and method course aims to introduce theories, models and methods in social work. It is integrated with the

first period of fieldwork practice so that the theoretical tasks during the practical placement build on and are connected to the content of the theory course. The integration will be used for clarifying the tension between theory and practice and for developing the ability to learn by integrating theory and practice. Ethics in social work occurs repeatedly as a constant strand in the teaching. This will help students focus on the ethical issues from a theoretical perspective when they are reflecting on how to handle situations that they face on their practice placement. This teaching structure will be used in both Terms Four and Five. There will be different pedagogical forms for working with ethical issues. Students might write their own case studies derived from the experience of their fieldwork practice, then analyse and discuss the ethical issues involved, both individually and with guidance as described in Chapter 2. Students will be asked to discuss and analyse professional ethical codes and try to link them to the different concrete situations they face. The students will do this on those days when they are recalled to the University. They will also have relevant discussions with their tutors at their practice placements. Part of the time during the recall days will be used for reflection on the role of the students in practice, on methods of handling difficult situations, and on decision-making. One way of working with this can be to use role-play in relation to professional conversations.

This social work and method course, integrated with fieldwork practice, will be examined by asking the students to describe and analyse the professional social work done at the practice placement. They should be able to clarify actual and specific problems connected to the practice placement, focusing on the handling and documentation of a case they have been involved in themselves, methods of assessing needs and capabilities, and ways of intervening with clients. Students should be able to make arguments concerning relevant legislation, theories, methods and models in social work. They are expected to reflect on the content of their analyses from an ethical perspective.

The social welfare legislation course

Having acquired this knowledge and skills, the students now face the next challenge – the social welfare legislation course, which is integrated with the second fieldwork practice period. The content covers the Social Services Act, the Human Rights Act, the Rights of the Child Act and other international conventions, legislation and regulations concerning support and services for the functionally disabled. The course also covers laws concerning restraint, Swedish laws for youth care, care of drug and alcohol abusers and psychiatric care. This legislation raises the ethical issue of voluntary versus compulsory social work. The principle of public access to official records, the Official Secrets Act and the Administrative Law, with regulations for workers in the public service, all constitute an important part of the course content and are also closely related to ethical issues.

The principal aim of this course is to develop further knowledge in social law and its application. Integrating the course with fieldwork practice aims to help the students to identify where they stand and how they should act in relation to legal issues in practice. There are four main areas that the students will focus on in this course, all of which include ethical dimensions:

1. The social worker has to know the law to be able to help the clients gain information about their rights and prospects as well as their duties and responsibilities. The crucial idea, especially of the legislation relating to the rights of severely disabled people, is that individuals themselves should demand their rights and support. The social worker is then the one who has to see if the applicant fits the criteria for the target group as defined by the law. If that is the case, the social worker should decide if and how the needs can be met according to the wishes of the person in need, balanced by what society is willing to offer. Handling such cases should raise awareness of the ethical issues arising along the whole chain of action, and of the need for ethical reflections by the social worker. During the course, the students' attention will be drawn to this and they will be asked to discuss how to decide what to do and for what reasons.

2. According to the Social Services Act, the local authority has a duty to provide information about rights and prospects in relation to the law and to make visits to get to know the needs of different groups in the local community (preventive work). Students should reflect on how to make good decisions when they have to choose between preventive work and having to act in crisis situations where the priority is not always obvious.

3. The Social Services Act is based on the idea of coping with individuals without intervening against their will, unless in exceptional circumstances where it may be necessary, for example, to take children into care or send a substance abuser for treatment. Ethical dilemmas often come up when the social worker has to interpret the norms of acceptable social behaviour on the one hand, and, on the other hand, has to listen to and interpret the needs of the individual. This raises the crucial question of finding the balance between voluntary and compulsory intervention.

4. The second fieldwork practice period will concentrate on the exercise of authority in social work, including the application of current legislation and formal regulations.

The Social Services Act in Sweden provides a framework within which services are provided for those in need. These services are delivered according to the policies of the local authorities and the decisions made by individual social workers. This gives social workers considerable responsibility for making judgements. The content and teaching of the course is intended to give the students the opportunity to begin acquiring the tools for this task. The experience of teaching students in this phase of the programme is that they are used to the discussion of ethics in social work in general to some extent, but less familiar with ethics related to the application of social law. The aim of the course at this level is to make the students aware of the questions and the importance of improving their ability to reflect upon the issues and conflicts that arise.

The students will be examined through an individual written assignment presented in a seminar. The task will be a project concerning social welfare legislation related to their fieldwork practice. The students are expected to make a report on applied legislation from a wide perspective, outlining arguments for different ways of interpreting and applying the legislation and international conventions. In this work the identification of ethical issues, ethical analysis and argument is important and obvious. The two aims of the examination are to measure the ability of the student in relation to the aims of the course and to give the students a learning opportunity through their work with the task. This is the phase when the student can complete the learning cycle as described by Thompson (2000).

Cumulative learning and improving ethical awareness

I would like to compare the expression, cumulative learning and developing ethical awareness of the students, with what Thompson (2000) writes about learning as an active process based on interaction between theory and practice. For that process, education has a responsibility to support students in different ways by meeting their needs for theoretical knowledge, for time to reflect, and for a structural model as a tool for analysis and practical work. What is meant by *cumulative* development of ethical awareness is that it is built up, step by step, based on the step before, to a higher level of integration of values, knowledge and skills. The first step entails the processing of experience through reflection that relates theory to practice. When students first go to fieldwork practice, they do not learn directly about ethics. They have to relate their experience to previous learning. This is why we want the students to bring examples from practice into the theoretical teaching, to give them the opportunity to 'process' the experience. For the next step, to make sense of the experience reflected upon in relation to theory, the student needs to put it back into practice. This will lead to an enlarged theory base for the student. The change will not happen immediately – it is a part of a process. The student has to work with this understanding over time and in different situations, for instance, by reading literature, through discussions, or in the examination task.

So far, students might have acquired knowledge, but they still have not learnt until that knowledge is tested and put into action. In this case, they have the advantage of being students in contrast to being qualified social workers. They have the opportunity to experiment, guided by a tutor, and in this way students start on the path to full learning. As Thompson asserts, learning is an active and person-centred process. Students are encouraged to take responsibility to use the period of practice to try out their theoretical understanding in the context of applied social work.

To continue the process of person-centred learning, the students then enter the phase when they ought to find out about what their needs for the rest of their study time are. They might suggest aims for further development or for specialist knowledge. This is possible in the last two terms of the programme. The optional course in Term Six is a course for specialisation in a particular area of social work. The study programme ends with a course entitled 'Social Work: Theory and Method', in which the student writes a dissertation worth 15 ECTS. The choice of subject is often a continuation of the specialisation, and the work with the dissertation gives the student a chance of using values, knowledge and skills in social work in a very personal way. Relating to Thompson's view of learning as an active and self-directed process, this final phase of their education could be the one when students complete the learning cycle. To write the dissertation, the student has to be self-directed and has to put theory to practice in a concrete way. It is hoped that this will lead to an increased understanding of social work as theory and practice.

Conclusions

Our work at Kalmar so far suggests that the integration of ethics teaching across the whole curriculum enables students to develop their learning about ethics progressively over time and in different contexts (classroom teaching about methods or the law, as well as in their practice placements). Our experience indicates, however, that it might be beneficial to introduce a specific course on ethics, perhaps in the second year of study. At this stage students have got enough knowledge to manage to raise questions about ethics in social work and therefore might be more motivated to take an active interest in the theoretical aspect of the subject, which they often find hard at an early stage. It could also be useful to hold literature-based seminars, to give opportunities for discussions based on a broader and deeper theoretical understanding connected to concrete situations. It is important that the ethical dimensions should be made explicit within all the courses, so students can recognise this element more clearly. This can be aided by requiring ethical perspectives in the examinations.

However, further evaluation is needed to enable us to assess the advantages and disadvantages of the integrated model of teaching ethics described here, and in particular its contribution to cumulative learning. In such an evaluation the students should be asked to describe their process of understanding ethical issues in theory and practice throughout their educational programme. The evaluation should also analyse how the students approach the ethical dimension in their examinations from a cumulative perspective.

Finally, it should be noted that in order to implement an integrated approach to ethics teaching effectively, it is crucial that the teachers on a programme are all committed to the project, and undertake regular ongoing discussions and evaluations of progress.

Appendix 9.1:
Examples of tasks given to students

1. Discussion questions about values in social work (1st year)

i) Values are often the basis of the attitudes that arise in the encounter with other people. The values mentioned below are indicated in different contexts and situations, as basic values in social work. They are, for example, central concepts in the Swedish Social Services Act.

Reflect first on what these values mean to you and then discuss them in the group:

- Social justice;
- Integrity;
- Self-determination;
- Equality;
- Respect for diversity and privacy.

ii) Values might be universal but they are always subjective. Discuss the basic values in social work, mentioned above, starting from the different perspectives below. Relate the discussion to one or more specific situations, if that is possible for you:

- Conflict between the values of the social worker and the client;
- Conflict between the values of the social worker and the employer.

Try to see what the consequences of the conflicts could be in a concrete situation and how they can affect encounters with the people you meet in social work.

2. Examination of the course in social work (1st year)

The task is to write a paper taking its starting point from the case you have already written in the earlier description of your 'naïve' or 'pre-training' conception of social work. You should write about the case at the individual/family level, group/organisation level and structural level. Try to examine different possible causes of the problem for the family, the effectiveness of different types of work, and the type of support and activities you would suggest. Give reasons for your opinion. Try also to explain in what way your original conception of social work has been confirmed or changed during the course. Give your references clearly, to show what is your own opinion and what has been taken from others.

Criteria for the grades:
Pass: The paper should show good basic knowledge in social work and be rooted in the course content and core literature.
Distinction: The criteria for a *pass* should be acquired. In addition the paper should demonstrate the ability for reflection, evaluation and critical analysis.
Fail: The standard for a pass has not been achieved and the task has to be resubmitted to be passed.

10.

Teaching ethics in an international context

Anne Liebing and Birgitte Møller

Introduction

This chapter is about the experiences of students and teachers from different European countries, who spent some eight days together in the Spring of 2002 carrying out an intensive teaching and learning programme about practical ethics in professional social educational work. The project was initiated and planned by a group of teachers from the European Social Ethics Project (ESEP), among them the authors of this chapter. After a presentation of the programme and its underlying educational principles, we explain what the students learned from their participation. Building mainly on the students' own reports, we show what happened to the students' awareness of and reflections on ethical issues, and demonstrate the importance of the international context as a main asset to the students' learning about ethics. Finally, we discuss our experiences as teachers in relation to the organization and planning of the programme.

The Intensive Programme (IP)

The title of the Intensive Programme was: 'Ethical challenges in modern social care work'. It was funded partly by the nine educational institutions involved and partly through the European Commission's Socrates Programme. The programme took place in the former castle of Wégimont in the countryside in East Belgium.

The participants were 46 students from seven European countries and their teachers, all members of the ESEP group (see Appendix 10.1). Participants came from as far north as

Tornio in Finland via Malmö in Sweden and Copenhagen in Denmark to Porto in Portugal in the south. From east to west, they came from Krakow in Poland via Osnabrück in Germany to Brussels in Belgium. The students shared a common interest in ethical issues. They were 2nd or 3rd year students of social educational work, and all had completed at least one period of practical internship in a social institution.

Principles and planning

In the planning of the programme we as teachers were greatly inspired by the theoretical basis and the approach to learning developed in the ESEP group, as exemplified in the earlier chapters in this book (see also Banks, 2001a; Nieweg 2001; Nøhr 2001). Most of the teachers involved already had practical experience of applying some of the methods in their own teaching. The idea of the Intensive Programme was to bring our students together in a common programme to get some experience as to what would happen to the students' awareness of and reflections on ethical issues when ethics was taught in an international, multi-cultural context.

The content and the planning of the programme was chosen according to three main educational principles:

1) *Priority should be given to students' own experience* – the focus should be on students' learning about ethics through their own reflections on practice, and not through a theoretical approach.

In the planning we thus chose that the dominant element in the programme should be group discussions by the students in international groups on cases from professional social practice. Less than one day of the programme was given to lectures from the teachers. Moreover these lectures were not meant to present theoretical perspectives on ethics, but rather to give inspiration and guidance to the groups. The lectures presented the basic concepts of ethical argumentation and introduced to the students the four step model for discussion and deciding in ethical dilemmas in social practice (see Chapter 5 for a variation on this model). Apart from this, the teachers' role was to ensure an optimal framework for the groups' work and to support the groups during the process.

2) *Students should be encouraged to be active* – the programme should be organised in such a way that students would be encouraged to take responsibility for their own learning process.

In the planning this principle was pursued mainly through the priority given to the group work and to the students' responsibility for their own group process. They were also responsible for writing a daily group report on what they had discussed and learned in the group during the day, and for a final report on the main discussions, conclusions and perspectives from the groups' work. The students had also been asked before the Intensive Programme to prepare themselves for the group work by reflecting on two given cases and to fill in their individual answers on the questionnaire (see Chapter 2, Appendix 2.1). Each student had also prepared a case from her/his own practice describing a situation, which they had themselves experienced as ethically problematic. The students were also responsible for preparing questions for visits to institutions.

3) *The programme should facilitate inter-cultural encounter* – the programme should present a good framework for exchange among the students from different cultural backgrounds.

In the planning the first whole day was allocated to presentations of the culture and social work in the different countries, the different educational programmes and educational institutions. In the formation of the working groups, much care was taken to ensure that they were internationally mixed with students from as many different countries/institutions as possible. Also the four groups visiting institutions were mixed this way. Each national group was responsible for the opening and closing of one 'national' day. The idea of the national day was that the teacher from the country in question was responsible for starting the day by introducing the day's programme and for organizing the necessary plenary sessions. Later in the day the students from the same country were responsible for starting the evening programme with one hour of common social/cultural activities. Students and the teacher from the country were afterwards responsible for running the bar throughout the evening's more informal gathering, often with music and dance.

The schedule for the Intensive Programme day-by-day was as follows:

Day 1: Arrival and welcoming programme.
Day 2: Presentation of participating countries and educations; formation of eight groups.
Day 3: Introduction to practical ethics. The mixed international groups start working.
Day 4: Group work on cases; preparation for visits.
Day 5: Visits to social institutions in three different cities.
Day 6: Group work on the visits and the students' own cases.
Day 7: Writing of the final group reports and evaluation.
Day 8: Departure.

What did the students learn from the Intensive Programme?

Our immediate impression during the week in Wégimont was that the programme was greatly inspiring to the students. In spite of the language difficulties, the students dedicated themselves to the group discussions with an open spirit and much energy. In the plenary sessions the groups presented interesting reflections inspired by the cases, and during the visits they engaged themselves actively in raising ethical questions and discussing with the social workers. Even through meals and the free time in the evenings, discussions on ethical issues were happening.

To get a more specific picture of what the students learned about 'ethics' from engaging themselves in this process, we will look to the students' own evaluations and to the conclusions and perspectives presented in the final reports from the working groups. The following quotations from the group reports cover some typical statements and point to three areas of learning: ethical awareness, ethical reflection and dealing with ethical problems and dilemmas in professional practice.

> In the future we will be more aware of ethical issues. We know how important it is to remember the ethics in everyday work. We have learned not to put our values on to others, but let them develop their own values, and to respect every individual and recognize that every one is different and should be treated individually.

> We learned to be more open-minded and to listen to other experiences and opinions, and not to be too quick in judging others.
> We became aware of different values, which made us more reflective.
> We learned to be more critical and to question our own work.

Ethical awareness

As stated above, the students conclude that they have developed a higher degree of ethical awareness – also referred to as 'ethical sensitivity' by some students. This awareness has to do with the realization that ethical issues are closely related to professional practice as part of everyday work. One student puts it this way: 'I found that there are ethical dilemmas in everyday life which I just might have passed without noticing.'

Moreover some students mention that through their own experiences in the group they have become aware of the special importance in social work of some specific ethical values such as tolerance and non-discrimination.

The students also point out that they have become aware of new ethical issues. Through examples from the visits and from the students' own personal cases they have come to realize that different ethical issues arise from different basic conditions for social work. For example, one group mentions that the case from a Portuguese student led to a discussion in the group about ethical problems caused by lack of resources in the social system. Several groups have become aware of ethical problems related to social work funded by private enterprises.

Another group concludes that they have become aware of the connection between ethics and legislation. For example ethical problems may come from legislation, which compromises important values in social work.

Several groups also reflect in their reports on the role of religion in social work, and on the ethical problems connected to social work within religious organisations.

Ethical reflection

Reading the students' reports there is no doubt that through the IP they have developed their ability for ethical reflection. Several groups conclude that they have realized that their own immediate points of view on the cases were quite narrow, but in the group they have 'helped each other to reflect on a higher level'. As examples, they mention that they have become aware that their own opinions may be influenced by emotions and by their own cultural norms and standards. In general the discussions have added more perspectives to the students' understanding of ethical problems in social work and more alternatives for dealing with ethical problems. They have come to 'regard ethical questions as complex.' They have become aware of the impact of socio-economic, political and cultural differences on defining what is an ethical problem and on the understanding of the essence of the problem, and so on. Thus they conclude – as shown in the reports quoted above – that ethical problems must be understood and dealt with in their context.

The group reports prove in different ways that ethical reflection has been an approach which inspires the students to critical reflection on social practice. Thus one group concludes directly: 'Actually the ethical way of thinking is a critical way of thinking, where you take nothing for granted.' All the group reports contain statements about having learned to question their own work as the group quoted above, for example: 'We learned to question our own work'; 'We now question issues that we might otherwise consider obvious.'

Dealing with ethical problems and dilemmas in professional practice

According to the students' reports and evaluations they have not only learned to be more aware of and reflect more deeply on ethical issues in practical social work. They are also convinced that they will in their future work act differently in situations involving ethical problems or dilemmas. One of the national summaries of the students' evaluations puts it this way: 'The students experience that they have gained a valuable insight in dealing with ethical dilemmas, got important 'tools' for solving ethical problems and to think and act in an ethical way in social work.'

It is important to note, that what they learned about 'dealing with ethical dilemmas' is not a specific way of acting. It is remarkable that the students' conclusions from the group work on the cases do not mention a concrete 'answer' or point to a specific course of action in the situation. Through the group process they seem to have become aware that 'acting in an ethical way' does not mean acting in one specific way, but to resolve on a course of action on a reflected basis taking into consideration the specific context. Likewise the 'tools' they mention are not tools or methods for acting in practice, but tools or methods for systematic reflections on practice. Several groups find the four step method useful, although time-consuming, for this purpose. It gave a 'clear structure to the discussion' and 'helped understand the need to ask the right questions'.

They have experienced that to ensure reflection that takes into consideration the complexity of an ethical problem or dilemma it is useful to engage in discussion with persons who have different experiences and backgrounds. They have also learned that some preconditions are crucial for this discussion to be an ethical communication: that the persons involved must be free, able and willing to speak openly and honestly, that they must listen with respect and be themselves open to questioning their own presumptions.

The students find that through the programme they have developed the necessary communicative and personal competences needed for engaging in ethical communication. The students find these skills will be of importance in their future practice, not only in communication with other professionals, but also for engaging in an ethical dialogue with clients with a different social and cultural background.

Learning ethics in an international context

The main objective for us in initiating the Intensive Programme was to see what happened to the students' awareness of and reflections on ethical issues, when ethics was taught in an international context. So far we have seen that the students do in fact heighten their ethical awareness and deepen their reflections on ethical issues and moreover the students develop important competences for dealing with ethical problems in practice and for engaging in ethical communication. To explore in which way the international context has contributed to this learning process, we shall again turn to the students' evaluations and the group reports.

The quotations below from the evaluation sheets represent rather well the points of view of many students. They show us that living and learning in the international context of the Intensive Programme in Wégimont has given the students some very important inter-cultural experiences. Furthermore, these experiences in turn have added something valuable to the students' learning about ethics. We will elaborate this point further through presenting three inter-cultural experiences and arguing their importance for learning ethics:

> It was amazing to discover how big differences there are between countries in every aspect of social care work, laws and regulations and in the ways of acting. The group discussions opened up totally new views, which really made me think more deeply. Totally new aspects surfaced. Working in an international group is a challenge. You have to accept everyone's opinion, even when it differs very much from your own.

> It is incredibly stimulating to discuss ethics with different persons with different aspects and perspectives. I have experienced that we through the discussions have developed each others' argument and thinking. Though we sometimes had totally opposite opinions, I all the time felt that we respected and inspired each other.

Experience of political, cultural and professional differences
As stated by both students above the experience of 'differences' has been very important to the students. Some students write that it has been interesting to experience differences 'in real and not only from TV' and that they have in general gained a 'wider horizon' and a 'broader view of the world'. The students have been greatly surprised to learn that such great differences exist between the European countries: differences in the basic socio-economic conditions and differences in social politics and in the social welfare systems on many levels. They have also become aware of differences in the cultural norms and standards in different parts of Europe as for what is a 'good family life', 'a good life for disabled persons' or 'sufficient child care'. The political and cultural differences in turn influence the professional traditions of social work.

The awareness of differences has opened the students' eyes to understanding that ethical issues are not the same everywhere, and that cthical problcms and dilemmas in social work are being understood and handled differently in the professional practice. Thus the international context has contributed in an important way to the students' awareness of new ethical issues. Discussing the cases with students from different countries has confronted them with completely opposite points of view and opinions on how to approach the ethical dilemmas in practice. They also realized that 'a person's opinion or choice of action is not merely a question of individual, personal choice, but has to do with cultural background and professional experiences'. In this way they have experienced that differences among the students themselves cannot and should not be ignored or easily argued away, but must be acknowledged and respected.

Experience that inter-cultural encounter and
understanding is possible
Differences are however not necessarily 'stimulating' as the student quoted above puts it. Often differences are seen rather as difficulties and obstacles. At the beginning of the group work many students found that language problems and cultural differences were barriers to the group process and made the work slow, shallow and frustrating. In this context, the most

important experience for the students may well have been the experience that it is in fact possible to overcome these barriers and to get to understand and learn from each other across language problems and cultural differences. As one group put it: 'At the start it looked hopeless, but at the end in our group we understood each other, but body language and patience were needed'.

The students became aware, however, that in order to reach across these barriers and establish the inter-cultural understanding you need not only the motivation for it but also some important communicative and personal competences. You must be willing and able to share your personal experiences and to express yourself clearly, and you must be open-minded and able to listen actively and with care and respect to others.

The interesting point is, that through the process of struggling actually to understand each other in the international groups, the students seem to have developed the personal and communicational competences needed to make the inter-cultural encounter possible. Because all students in a group had different backgrounds and spoke in a foreign language, they could not take for granted that they would immediately understand each other correctly. Consequently the students had to engage themselves in a slow and careful communication process. Thus the international context gave them the possibility to learn to listen more carefully, ask more questions and have an open attitude to acknowledging differences. They also learned to express themselves more clearly and creatively, using more body language and illustrating their statements by using metaphors, models or examples.

One group describes this process in their report in this way:

> We have spent a lot of time translating and explaining, so the process has been a bit slow but also more exciting and interesting. It takes a lot of patience and tolerance, and we have had to be more concentrated during the discussions.

Another group concludes: 'The language difficulties made us more flexible and helped to think in alternatives. It made us help each other to explain and understand.'

These personal and communicational competences and the

open attitude developed through the group process are not only needed to establish inter-cultural encounter and communication. They are the very same skills we presented earlier in this chapter as the necessary preconditions for engaging in ethical communication. Thus the international context of the programme and the process of struggling to overcome the language barriers seems to be the crucial factor for the students to develop their abilities for ethical communication and thus their ability to deal with ethical problems and dilemmas in a reflective way.

Experience that differences can be inspiring and enriching

If the students' first inter-cultural experience is the realization that important differences exist, and the second that inter-cultural understanding and communication is possible, then the third experience is, that under these conditions, differences in background and approach can be turned from an obstacle into an asset.

As a preparation for the Intensive Programme, some of the students had taken part in group discussions about the cases presented in the questionnaire in their home country. Although they find that this group work added new aspects to their own individual understanding of the ethical dilemmas in the cases, they also find that compared with the international group the 'home' group reached consensus too quickly. In their opinion, the discussion with students from different European countries is more inspiring, as it opens wider perspectives, presents more interesting ideas and points to new alternatives for dealing with the ethical dilemmas in practice.

In the quotations above (and others like them) the main point is that discussing practical ethics with students from different backgrounds adds more complexity to their understanding of ethical issues and enriches and deepens their ethical reflections. Once the students realize that the differences among them must be acknowledged and respected and that inter-cultural understanding is possible, they find that differences are 'incredibly stimulating'. They come to 'think more deeply' and they 'develop each others' argument and thinking'. Another group concludes: 'The deeper we got into the discussion the more important questions came up.'

The international context also enhances the students' ability for critical reflection on their own practice. Through the awareness of political differences and cultural diversity the students become aware that also their own opinions and arguments may be questioned as based on 'local' political, cultural and professional traditions.

Teaching ethics in an international context

As is obvious from the presentation above, our experiences from bringing together students and teachers from different European countries for this Intensive Programme on ethics are very positive. As we have shown, the process of living and learning in an international and multi-cultural context has in several important ways added to the students' learning. In this last part of the chapter we shall give more attention to what we learned as teachers and elaborate on our experiences from organizing and planning the programme. Thus we hope that our experiences may provide some useful inspiration to colleagues who may be considering whether to engage in similar projects.

First and foremost we must point to the small international working groups as the place for the most important learning for the students for the reasons described above. A successful outcome of working in groups is, however, not guaranteed. Through the Intensive Programme we have also learned that there are some necessary preconditions for the group work. First, it is of great importance to the students' inter-cultural experiences that no compromises are made regarding the international and multi-cultural formation of the groups. Second, it is crucial that we stay true in organizing the programme to the basic educational principles of keeping the focus on the students' learning process and on their own active contribution to and responsibility for the process. In other words, the teachers must stick to the role of organizing beforehand the best possible framework for the students' learning process, and ensuring in the course of the programme the necessary support, inspiration and guidance to the groups. Below we shall elaborate these points further and share our experiences concerning the organizing and planning of a programme according to these principles.

Ensuring and supporting the group process

To ensure good working conditions and the optimal learning process for the groups, the following factors must be considered in the planning:

1. *Formation of the groups* – The groups must be internationally mixed to represent the greatest possible diversity. As mentioned above, differences in backgrounds and experiences in the group of students may be the foremost precondition for critical reflection and for developing the ability for ethical communication. The groups should be small (5-6 students). In a small group it is easier to establish an open atmosphere, in which it is safe to share personal opinions and emotions and to question one's own points of view. In a small group everybody can contribute with their experiences and take part in the discussion. Students are also challenged to speak, even if they do not know the language very well, and thus they develop their communication skills.

2. *Language* – The students in the group should be able to communicate in a basic way in the same language. If the students have to translate between different languages while working in the group, there is a risk that the exchange stays too slow and shallow and thus is frustrating for the students. Consequently the language problems may become a barrier for reaching the point where diversity becomes inspiring and deepens the reflections. On the other hand, it is not important that the students speak the language fluently. On the contrary, in our experience it is an advantage in the process that nobody speaks in their mother tongue. Having to be open for understanding and to listen carefully is an asset to develop the awareness, attitudes and the skills needed for engaging in an ethical discussion.

3. *Working with cases* – It is important that the students have examples from professional practice as a basis for their

group discussions. We have found that practical examples in the form of cases – fictional and authentic – stimulate the group discussions, as do visits to social institutions and discussions with the staff about the ethical problems in their practice. Advantages and disadvantages in using fictional and authentic cases have been discussed in Chapter 2 of this book. Fictional or pre-prepared real cases have the advantage that the students can prepare beforehand their individual points of view on the same case, which is a good starting point for comparison and discussion. On the other hand, using the students' own cases presents a greater range of different situations and conditions for social work.

4. *Teacher's support for the group process* – The same teacher should be attached to the group throughout the programme. The students are primarily responsible for the group process and for writing the group reports; the teacher's role is to give supervision, guidance and support to the process. The teacher should be present at the first meeting, when the group establishes itself and initiates their work. The teacher should be present in the group at the beginning of each group session. In the course of the programme the teacher should be attentive to the group process, respect the decisions of the group and be available when the students decide that they need support.

5. *Supporting the group process by providing specific working tools* – In our experience it may be helpful to the group process to present to the groups some working tools. In the Intensive Programme we presented to the students the 'four steps method' (a variation of the seven-step approach described in Chapter 6). Several groups found this method helpful in that it gave structure to their discussion of the cases. Another useful tool is to give general guidelines for writing the reports and guidelines to support the group's decision about norms for their group process. It is important, however, that the supervisor respects the group's own choice of working method.

6. *Group reports* – Writing daily reports of the main issues from the group discussions is very demanding for the students, but supportive to the group process. It helps maintain a continuous group work and to extract from different opinions and reflections some main conclusions. The fact that the final group reports are used as official documentation of the programme adds importance and seriousness to the students' work and enhances the students' responsibility.

7. *Time for the group process* – The most important precondition for the group process is to have enough time. It takes time to establish an atmosphere of confidence in the group and it takes time to understand each other when speaking in a foreign language. Reflections need time to deepen and the writing of reports takes time. Consequently it is important not to overload the groups with tasks. In the planning the teachers should aim at minimizing the number of cases to be discussed and the number of methods introduced.

Ensuring the inter-cultural exchange in the general planning

Finally we will give some attention to the experiences about the planning of the overall framework of the programme. Although we find that the small groups are crucial for the inter-cultural experiences, some general elements in the programme as a whole played an important part in making way for these experiences.

As we have argued above, two conditions are needed in order that the international context shall be inspiring and enriching for the students: they must experience that differences are real and must be taken seriously, *and* they must experience that it is possible to understand each other in spite of them. Consequently we must insist on both in the general planning.

On the one hand we must make an effort to demonstrate the international differences and the cultural diversity among the participants – for example, through the presentations of the different countries, social work and educational institutions, and through the national days and evenings throughout the programme. On the other hand it is also important to create an open atmosphere and a communal spirit across the national groups – for example, through insisting on communal social life even during the evenings' leisure time.

Another issue to consider is the teachers' role as possible models for inter-cultural encounter and cooperation. During the communal life of the Intensive Programme it became quite obvious to the students that the group of teachers was also struggling with language problems and with different approaches caused by different academic backgrounds. Nevertheless we brought with us the common experiences from cooperating in the ESEP group, and the very fact that we initiated and carried through the programme together was a daily illustration that, in spite of great differences in teaching and learning traditions, it is not only possible but greatly stimulating to teach ethics together in an international community.

Conclusions

We shall conclude this chapter with a small anecdote from the last day of group work in Wégimont. The group in question is discussing their main conclusions and perspectives for the final report. As her contribution a Portuguese student presents with warm enthusiasm and more or less the following words this mental picture:

> I feel that I have become a rich woman now. When I come home, I shall still have this group inside my head. After this I shall not act immediately, when I meet a difficult situation or an ethical dilemma in my practice. Instead I shall discuss the situation with my group inside my head. I shall say to myself: What would the Finnish student say or do in this situation? And what would be the point of view of the Belgian student? How would the Danish student react to this problem, and what would the German student consider important? In this way I would be able to think of many important aspects and many different alternatives, before I decide how to act in practice.

This anecdote illustrates very nicely that this student has learned something of importance for her future practice about how to deal with ethical dilemmas through ethical reflection. It also illustrates how closely her insights about ethics are related to the process of inter-cultural exchange and discussion in the group. Last but not least it demonstrates how well the main points of this chapter can be expressed with a limited vocabulary supplied with the necessary communicational creativity.

Acknowledgements

We would like to express our thanks to all the participating students and staff who contributed to the IP and whose experiences and reports we have drawn upon.

Appendix 10.1:
List of teachers and schools participating in the Intensive Programme

Anna Zielinska	University of Krakow, Poland
Anne Liebing	Roskilde Pædagogseminarium, Denmark
Birgitte Møller	Københavns Socialpædagogiske Seminarium, Denmark
Henk Goovaerts	Katholieke Hogeschool Limburg, Belgium
François Gillet	Haute Ecole de Bruxelles, Belgium
Isabel Baptista	Universidade Portucalense, Porto, Portugal
Jochen Windheuser	Katholische Fachhochschule Norddeutschland, Germany
Katariina Ylipahkala	Humanities Polytechnic, Tornio, Finland
Karin Stenberg and Lars Plantin	Malmö Högskola, Sweden

11.

Some useful literature for teaching professional ethics

Wilfred Diekmann

Introduction

In this publication about teaching methods we should not neglect one of the most common 'tools' in teaching, namely, literature. In the European Social Ethics Project we have been interested in the books used by colleagues. In this chapter you will find reference to some of the literature used by teachers in ten countries: Belgium, Denmark, England, Finland, France, Germany, the Netherlands, Portugal, Sweden and Switzerland. Eight languages are involved. We made a distinction between books useful for students and books colleagues find useful in teaching preparation. Some websites are also included. A short comment on the book or site is added.

The list presented here is very limited in its purpose and design:

- The focus is on literature found useful in teaching and learning about ethics in relation to the social professions, thus only few general works about ethics are included;
- These are books used by *some* teachers in *some* countries/languages – so the selection is necessarily a partial one;
- We limited the number of books to 5-10 in every language;
- The list comprises books and some internet sites, no reviews or journal articles.

One step still to be made by the ESEP in the future is to discuss the role of books in teaching ethics. This will involve considering questions such as:

- What is the role and what could or should be the role of books in teaching practical ethics for the social professions? How can books be useful? What are the limitations and even disadvantages?
- What are criteria for a useful book in this context?
- Do the listed books meet those criteria and to what extent?

So this list of teachers' recommendations should be seen as a beginning.

Danish

Books useful for students

Andersen, John (1999) *Den enkelte og det fælles. Om etik, omsorg og forebyggelse,* København, BUPL.
(*The individual and the collective. On ethics, care and prevention.* About ethics in working with children and young people based on projects in several day-care institutions.)

Flindt Pedersen, Jette (1992) *Etik – ja tak. Brugerens oplevelse af det sociale system.* København, Socialpædagogisk Bibliotek Munksgaard.
(*Ethics – Yes please. How users experience the social system.* It is often a problem that there is no conscious ethical attitude in the organisation of social work. The book gives ideas as how to qualify the meeting between human beings in social work.)

Johansson, Eva (2002) *Små børns etik,* København, Hans Reitzels Forlag.
(*The ethics of young children.* Translated from Swedish. The book is about the interactions between the youngest children in the kindergarten: their ethics, the values and norms and how these are expressed. The book is built on a study of a group of children and their ways of experiencing the world through their bodies. It develops theories and discusses international research on the moral development of children.)

Lingås, Lars Gunnar (1999) *Etik for social - og sundhedsarbejdere. En grundbog,* København, Hans Reitzels Forlag.
(*Ethics for social workers and health care workers.* Translated from Norwegian: *Etikk og verdivalg i helse- og socialfag.* The book introduces various ethical approaches in professional social work and

health work. Includes the codes of ethics for nurses and for social workers.)

Madsen, Bent (1993) *Socialpædagogik og samfundsforvandling*, København, Munksgaard.

(*Social pedagogics and the changing of society*. The book discusses how the theory and praxis of social care work can adjust to the changing society. It gives new perspectives on the education and ethics raised by the paradoxes in social work.)

Books useful for teachers

Thomassen, Niels (1993) *Etik. En introduktion*, København, Filosofi, Gyldendal.

(A basic introduction to different theories of ethics. Includes a proposal for a course in ethics.)

Thyssen, Ole (1997) *Værdiledelse. Om organisationer og etik*, København, Gyldendal.

(*Value-management. On organisations and ethics*. Ethical problems in organisations. It is often expected that ethics can give authoritarian answers about right and wrong. But how can right and wrong be discussed in a society where each individual can choose their lifestyle? Ethics is seen as a culture of dialogue.)

Dutch

Books useful for students

Ebskamp, J. and Kroon, H. (1997) *Beroepsethiek voor SPH*, Baarn, Uitgeverij Intro.

(A short introduction to (professional) ethics and ethical reasoning followed by several ethical aspects of social educational care work.)

Janssen, Jan, H.G. (2001) *De nieuwe code gedecodeerd. Maatschappelijk werk en beroepsethiek*, (1991 – 2001), Baarn, HB-uitgevers.

(Explanation of the professional code of ethics for social workers.)

Reijen, M. van (1999) *Filosofie en hulpverlening 1, wijsgerige kernbegrippen*, Baarn, Nelissen.

(A book on philosophy and the helping-professions. Basic themes are human freedom, willing and choosing and social philosophy in human relations, values and norms, power, etc.)

Savornin Lohman, J. de and Raaff, H. (2001) *In de frontlinie tussen hulp en recht*, Bussum, Uitgeverij Coutinho.
(This book is about the tension between ethics of justice and ethics of care. The 'frontier worker' (for example: social worker) has to find a balance between them.)

Timmer, Sylvia, (1998) (ed) *Tijd voor ethiek. Handreikingen voor ethische vragen in de praktijk van maatschappelijk werkers,* Bussum, Uitgeverij Coutinho.
(This book is an edited book with articles on several ethical themes in the practice of social workers.)

Books useful for teachers
Kessels, J. (1997) *Socrates op de markt: Filosofie in bedrijf,* Amsterdam, Boom.
(A book on the use of philosophical reasoning in everyday life, especially the use in corporate decision making and targeting. Gives elaborate explanation of the practical use of Socratic dialogue in consultancy.)

Kunneman, H. (1996) *Van theemutscultuur naar walkman-ego, Contouren van postmoderne individualiteit,* Amsterdam/Meppel, Boom.
(In this book Kunneman develops his theory of 'normative professionalism', which is always a personal mix of 'technical', 'normative reflective' and communicative aspects.)

Widdershoven, G. (2000) *Ethiek in de kliniek, Hedendaagse benaderingen in de gezondheidsethiek,* Amsterdam/Meppel, Boom.
(An overview of six contemporary approaches in health care ethics. Very useful for the social professions.)

English
Books useful for students
Banks, S. (1999) (ed) *Ethical Issues in Youth Work,* London, Routledge.
(A varied collection of chapters by different authors on a range of themes, including: confidentiality, the ethics of funding, controlling young people, religious conversion, young people's rights and youth workers as 'friends'.)

Banks, S. (2001) *Ethics and Values in Social Work*, 2nd edition, Basingstoke, Palgrave.

(A brief introduction to ethical theories, along with discussions of ethical codes and dilemmas in practice.)

Thompson, M. (1999) *Ethical Theory*, London, Hodder and Stoughton.

(Covers the main ethical theories briefly. Students find this a useful basic introduction.)

Books useful for teachers

Boss, J. (1998) *Ethics for Life: An Interdisciplinary and Multi-Cultural Introduction*, Mayfield, Mountain View, CA.

(Useful background on various ethical theories, written in clear, practical style.)

Gambrill, E. and Pruger, R. (1997) (ed) *Controversial Issues in Social Work Ethics, Values, and Obligations*, Berkeley, University of California.

(Debates several issues such as: the role of professional codes of ethics, professional education and training and the responsibility of practitioners.)

Kuhse, H. and Singer, P. (1999) (eds), *Bioethics: An Anthology*, Oxford, Blackwell.

(Useful collection of articles on a variety of topics, focusing on bioethics.)

LaFollette, H. (ed) (1997) *Ethics in Practice: An Anthology*, Oxford, Blackwell.

(Useful collection of articles on a variety of topics.)

Finnish

Books useful for students

Pietarinen, Juhani (1998) *Etiikan teorioita*, Helsinki, Gaudeamus.

(Some basic theories about ethics, philosophical point of view.)

Lindqvist, Martti (2000) *Tässä seison: uskottavan etiikan jäljillä*, Helsinki, Otava.

(Reflections on ethical thinking and practice.)

Juha Hamalainen and Pauli Niemela (1993) *Sosiaalian etiikka*, Helsinki,WSOY.

(Ethics of social work. Important reading for students and also professionals in the field of social work.)

Books useful for teachers
Ollila, Maija-Riitta (2002) *Erheitä ja virheitä*, Helsinki, WSOY.

(Philosophical reading about ethics and humanity.)

Patry, Jean-Luc and Lehtovaara, Jorma (eds) (1999) *European perspectives on teacher ethics,* Tampere, Tampereen yliopisto/University of Tampere.

(Some discussions and results about different perspectives on teacher ethics and consequences in Europe.)

French

Books useful for students
Fourez, G. (1990) *Eduquer / Écoles éthiques et sociétés,* Belgium, De Boeck Université.

(A good introduction to the link between what happens in several educational institutions and a possible ethical reflection on the choice of ways of educating.)

Books useful for teachers
Comte-Sponville, André (1998) *Pensées sur la morale*, Paris, éditions Albin Michel.

(This is a book of quotations and it allows students to discuss different points of view in ethics.)

Lalose, J.P. (1995) *Ethique et Vérité*, Paris, L'Harmattan.

(A stimulating reflection about the place of ethics in philosophy.)

Morissette, D. (1989) *Enseigner des attitudes,* Belgium, De Boeck Université.

(A good way of connecting the difficulty of changing some aspects of our behaviour in personal as well as in professional life.)

Rouzel, Joseph (1997) *Le travail d'Education spécialisé, éthique et pratique*, Dunod.

(Rouzel is social educator and psychoanalyst. He gives us a good reflection about practical ethics in the everyday life of a social worker.)

Vergez, A. and Huisman, D. (1987) *Nouveau cours de philo,* Paris, Fernand Nathan.
(A manual of philosophy with clear and interesting sequences about ethics.)

German
Books useful for students
Antor, G. and Bleidick, U. (2000) *Behindertenpädagogik als angewandte Ethik,* Stuttgart, Kohlhammer.
(Presentation and discussion of specific problems of disability from an ethical point of view.)

Baum, U. (1996) *Ethik sozialer Berufe,* Paderborn, UTB 1918.
(A short introduction to the terminology of ethics and its relation to specific problems emerging in working fields of social professions.)

Martin, E. (2001) *Sozialpädagogische Berufsethik. Auf der Suche nach dem richtigen Handeln,* Weinheim, Juventa.
(A contribution to ethical explications and reflections on problems emerging in modern societies in the context of social professions.)

Books useful for teachers
Engelke, Ernst (1998) *Theorien der Sozialen Arbeit,* Freiburg im Breisgau, Lambertus Verlag.
(An historical orientated survey of different approaches to social work from Jean J. Rousseau to Silvia Staub-Bernasconi.)

Moebius, St. (2001) *Postmoderne Ethik und Sozialität,* Stuttgart, Ibidem
(A contribution to deliberations concerning the social and ethical responsibility under conditions of globalisation and individualisation.)

Nida-Rümelin, J. (1996) *Angewandte Ethik. Die Bereichsethiken und ihre theoretische Fundierung. Handbuch,* Stuttgart, Kröner.
(A handbook providing a survey and foundation of specific ethical approaches relevant for different working fields.)

Unterholzner, B. (2000) *Grundfragen philosophischer Ethik,* Donauwörth, Auer Verlag.
(Crucial questions from the field of philosophical ethics; assumes little knowledge of philosophy.)

Portuguese

Books useful for students and teachers

Baptista, Isabel (1998) *Ética e Educação,* Porto, Portucalense.
(A Levinasian approach to professional ethics covering the importance of the face to face encounter; ethics of hospitality; the need of balance between ethical principles and subjectivity; enigma; the asymmetry of ethical relations; the exigency of dialogue.)

Carvalho, Adalberto Dias (1992) *A educação como projecto antropológico,* Porto, Afrontamento.
(Education as practical anthropology; the role of utopias in the conception of educational projects)

Swedish

Books useful for students

Henriksen, J-O. and Vetlesen, A. J. (2001) *Etik i arbete med människor,* Lund, Studentlitteratur.
(A basic book. Introduction to different ethical approaches and a concrete model for working with ethical issues in human services work.)

Meuwisse, A., Sunesson, S. and Swärd, H. (ed.) (2000) *Socialt Arbete. En grundbok,* Stockholm, Natur och Kultur.
(The book as a whole is about different perspectives on social work. Two useful chapters concerning ethics are about values and norms in social work and the ethics of practice of research.)

Books useful for teachers

Ronnby, A. (ed) (1999) *Etik och idéhistoria i socialt arbete,* Stockholm, Socionomen.
(The book throws light upon the history of ideas and ethics in the social policy and in social work and debates several themes about the value of professional codes of ethics.)

Some websites

http://www.durham.ac.uk/community.youth/ESEP/ESEP/htm
(The website of the European Social Ethics Project. It is under construction and contains some downloadable materials and articles.)

http://www.ethics.ubc.ca/
(Centre for Applied Ethics at University of British Columbia. This site includes research, research projects and links to resources and websites for applied ethics, including professional ethics.)

http://www.ethics.ubc.ca/mcdonald/decisions.html
(A useful framework for Ethical Decision-Making)

http://www.professionalethics.ca/
(Resources on professional ethics in Canada and worldwide.)

http://www.globalethics.org/
(Institute for Global Ethics, has a database of dilemmas in ordinary life.)

http://www.utm.edu/research/iep/
(The Internet Encyclopedia of Philosophy – has an A-Z of key words and philosophers, including moral philosophers and ethical theory.)

http://www.dbsh.de/html/prinzipien.html
(Berufsethische Prinzipien des DBSH und Ethische Grundlagen der Sozialen Arbeit – Prinzipien und Standards. German Professional Association for Social Work and Social Pedagogues; the ethical basis of social work - principles and standards.)

References

Banks, S. and Williams, R. (1999) 'The personal and the professional: perspectives from European social education students', *Social Work in Europe*, vol. 6, no. 3, pp. 52-61.

Banks, S. (2001a) 'Ethical dilemmas for the social professions: work in progress with social education students in Europe', *European Journal of Social Education*, no. 1, pp. 1-16.

Banks, S. (2001b) *Ethics and Values in Social Work*, 2nd edition, Basingstoke, Palgrave.

Birdwhistell, R. (1973) *Kinesics and Context: Essays on Body-Motion Communication*, Harmondsworth, Penguin.

Blennberger, E. (2000) 'Etik för socialt arbete' in A. Meeuwisse, S. Sunesson and H. Swärd (eds) *Socialt arbete: En grundbok*, Stockholm, Natur och Kultur, pp. 217-238. (Social work: A textbook)

Boal, A. (1992) *Games for Actors and Non-Actors*, translated by Adrian Jackson, London, Routledge.

Boal, A. (1995) *The Rainbow of Desire: the Boal method of theatre and therapy*, translated by Adrian Jackson, London, Routledge.

Bouquet, B. (1999) 'De l'éthique personelle à une éthique professionelle', *EMPAN*, no. 36, pp. 27-33. (From personal ethics to a professional ethics)

Callahan, J. (1998) 'From the "Applied" to the Practical:Teaching Ethics for Use', in K. Tziporah (ed), *In the Socratic Tradition: Essays on Teaching Philosophy*, Lanham, Maryland, Rowman & Littlefield, pp. 57-70.

Carlsmith, C. (1994) 'An "Academical Notebook"', http://www.virginia.edu/~trc/tcacabk.htm

Chambers, T. (1997) 'What to Expect from an Ethics Case (and What it Expects from You)' in H. Nelson (ed), *Stories and their limits: narrative approaches to bioethics*, New York and London, Routledge, pp. 171-184.

Cohn, R. (1976) TCI, Theme Centered Interaction (TZI, Themazentered Interaktion), http://www.tu-berlin.de/fak8/ifg/psychologie/legewie/Mod-engl-kurz.pdf

Dart, B. et al. (1998) 'Change in knowledge of learning and teaching through journal writing', *Research Papers in Education*, vol.13, no. 3, pp. 291-318.

De Jonghe, E.(1995) *Ethiek voor maatschappelijk werkers, Een methodische aanpak van morele dilemmas,* Bussum, Cootinho. (Ethics for social care workers, a methodological approach through moral dilemmas)

Department of Health and Behavioural Sciences (2000) *Study programme for social work programme, 210 ECTS,* Kalmar, University of Kalmar.

Dominelli, L. (1997) *Anti-racist social work,* London, Macmillan.

Dörner, D. (1992) *Die Logik des Mißlingens: Strategisches Denken in komplexen Situationen,* Reinbek, Rowohlt.

Dörner, D. (1996) *The logic of failure: Recognizing and avoiding error in complex situations,* Reading, Mass., Addison-Wesley (translation of Dörner 1992).

Dörner, D., Kreuzig, H.W., Reither, F. and Stäudel, Th. (1994) *Lohhausen: Vom Umgang mit Unbestimmtheit und Komplexität,* Bern, Hans Huber. (Lohhausen: On dealing with uncertainty and complexity)

Dörner, D. and Schaub, H. (1994) 'Errors in planning and decision-making and the nature of human information processing', *Applied Psychology,* vol. 43, pp. 433-453.

Dörner, D. and Wearing, A. (1995) 'Complex problem solving: Toward a (computer simulated) theory' in P. Frensch and J. Funke (eds) *Complex problem solving: The European perspective,* Hillsdale N.J., Erlbaum, pp. 65-99.

Ebskamp, J.and Kroon, H. (1990) *Ethisch leren denken in de hulpverlening, verzorging en dienstverlening,* Nijkerk. (Learning to think ethically in social care, nursing and services)

Ebskamp, J. and Kroon, H. (1994) *Beroepsethiek voor sociale en pedagogische hulpverlening,* Nijkerk, Intro. (Professional ethics for social care work)

Franke, W. and Sander-Franke, U. (1998) *Methodisches Lösen sozialer Probleme,* Köln, Fortis FH. (Solving social problems methodologically)

Gilligan, C. (1982) *In a Different Voice: Psychological Theory and Women's Development,* Cambridge, Mass., Harvard University Press.

Goffman, E. (1971) *Relations in Public: Microstudies of the Public Order,* Harmondsworth, Penguin.

Goodwin, C. (1981) *Conversational Organization: Interaction between Speakers and Hearers,* Academic Press, New York and London.

Hall, C., Sarangi, S. and Slembrouck, S. (1997) 'Moral Construction in social work discourse', in B.-L. Gunnarsson, P. Linell and B. Nordberg (eds), *The Construction of Professional Discourse*, London, Longman, pp. 265-291.

Hatton, N. and Smith, D. (1995) 'Reflection in teacher education – towards definition and implementation', *Teaching and Teacher Education*, vol. 11, no. 1, pp. 33-49.

Henriksen, J-O. and Vetlesen, A.J. (2001) *Etik i arbete med människor*, Lund, Studentlitteratur. (Ethics in work with people)

Hooft, S. van, (2001a) 'Socratic Dialogue as collegial reasoning', *Practical Philosophy,* vol. 2, http://members.aol.com/ PracticalPhilo/Volume2Articles/VanHooft.html

Hooft, S. van (2001b) 'What is self-fulfilment? A report on a Socratic Dialogue', *Practical Philosophy,* vol. 4:1, pp 47-55, http://www.practical-philosophy.org.uk

Houdart, B. (1997) 'Werken met een ethisch stappenplan' *C.E.Z.* (Cahier voor Ethiek en Zingevingsvragen), no. 5. (Working with an ethical staged-plan)

Kant, I. (1964) *Groundwork of the Metaphysics of Morals*, New York, Harper Row.

Kessels, J. (1997), *Socrates op de Markt: Filosofie in Bedrijf,* Amsterdam, Boom. (Socrates in the Market Place: Philosophy in a Business Environment)

Kolb, D. (1984) *Experiential Learning,* Englewood Cliffs, New Jersey, Prentice Hall.

Levinas, E. (1984) *Justifications de l'éthique*, Bruxelles, Edition de l'Université de Bruxelles. (Justifications of ethics)

Levinas, E. (1989) 'Ethics as First Philosophy, translated by Seán Hand', in S. Hand (ed), *The Levinas Reader*, Oxford, Blackwell, pp. 75-87.

Levy, C. (1993) *Social Work Ethics on the Line*, Binghampton, New York, The Haworth Press.

Løgstrup, K. (1997) *The Ethical Demand*, Notre Dame, Ind., University of Notre Dame Press.

Miller, G.A., Galanter, S. and Pribram, K. (1960): *Plans and the structure of behavior*, New York, Holt, Rinehart & Winston.

Mill, J.S. (1972) *Utilitarianism, On Liberty, and Considerations on Representative Government*, London, Dent.

Moon, J. (1999) *Learning Journals: A Handbook for Academics, Students and Professional Development*, London, Kogan Page.

Nelson, L. and Kessels, J. (1994), *De socratische methode* Amsterdam, Boom. (The Socratic method)

Nieweg, M. (2001) 'Learning to reflect: a practical theory on teaching', *European Journal of Social Education*, vol. 1, pp. 29-41.

Noddings, N. (1984) *Caring: A Feminine Approach to Ethics and Moral Education*, Berkeley and Los Angeles, University of California Press.

Nøhr, K. (2001) 'Learning to learn: reflections on students' learning processes in project work', *European Journal of Social Education*, vol. 1, pp. 17-27.

Possehl, K. (1993) *Methoden der Sozialarbeit,* Frankfurt am Main, Peter Lang. (Methods of social work)

Reamer, F. (1997) 'Debates about Professional Education and Training', in E. Gambrill and R. Pruger (eds) *Controversial Issues in Social Work: ethics, values, and obligations,* Berkeley, University of California, pp. 164-175.

Reece, I. and Walker, S. (2000) *Teaching, Training and Learning: A Practical Guide*, Sunderland, BEP.

Reither, F. (1997) *Komplexitätsmanagement. Denken und Handeln in komplexen Situationen,* München, Gerling. (Management of complexity. Thinking and acting in complex situations)

Rest, J. (1994) 'Background: Theory and Research', in J. Rest and D. Narváez (eds), *Moral Development in the Professions: Psychology and Applied Ethics*, Hillsdale, New Jersey, Lawrence Erlbaum Associates, pp. 1-26.

Richardson, L. (1994) 'Writing. A method of inquiry' in N. Denzin and Y. Lincoln (eds) *Handbook of Qualitative Research*, London, Sage.

Schön, D. (1983) *The Reflective Practitioner*, San Francisco, Jossey-Bass.

Schön, D. (1987) *Educating the Reflective Practitioner: Towards a New Design for Teaching and Learning*, San Francisco, Jossey-Bass.

Schön, D. (1991) *The Reflective Practitioner: How Professionals Think in Action*, (1st pub. 1983) paperback edn, Aldershot, Avebury/Ashgate.

Sevenhuijsen, S. (1996) *Oordelen met zorg: Feministische beschouwingen over recht, moraal en politiek*, Amsterdam, Uitgeverij Boom.

Sevenhuijsen, S. (1998) *Citizenship and the Ethics of Care: Feminist Considerations on Justice, Morality and Politics*, London, Routledge. (Translation of Sevenhuijsen 1996)

Siegel, D.H. (1984) 'Defining empirically based practice', *Social Work*, vol. 29, pp. 325-331.

Smith, M. (1994) *Local Education: community, conversation, praxis*, Buckingham, Open University Press.

Sommer D. (1993) *The reconstruction of Childhood*, Aarhus, Denmark, Institute of Psychology, University of Aarhus.

Sparkes-Langer, G. and Colton, A. (1991) 'Synthesis of research on teachers' reflective thinking', *Educational Leadership*, March, pp. 23-32.

Taylor, C. and White, S. (2000) *Practising Reflexivity in Health and Welfare: Making Knowledge*, Buckingham, Open University Press.

Ten Have, P. (1999) *Doing Conversation Analysis: A Practical Guide*, London, Sage.

Thompson, N. (2000) *Theory and practice in human services*, 2nd edition, Buckingham, Open University Press.

Tronto, J. (1993) *Moral Boundaries: A Political Argument for an Ethic of Care*, London, Routledge.

Van Manen, M. (1977) 'Linking ways of knowing and ways of being', *Curriculum Inquiry*, vol. 6, pp. 205-8.

Vetlesen, A. (1994) *Perception, Empathy and Judgment: An Inquiry into the Preconditions of Moral Performance*, University Park, Pennsylvania, The Pennsylvania State University Press.

Werthmüller, H.(1993) *Menschlich Lernen*, Meilen, Switzerland, SI TZT-Verlag. (Human Learning)

Wilde, P. and Wilson, M. (2001) *Building Practitioner Strengths: Reflecting on Community Development Practice*, London, Community Development Foundation.

Zentrale Beratungsstelle Osnabrück (ed) (1999) *Jeder Mensch braucht ein Zuhause: Jahresbericht 1998*, Osnabrück, Selbstverlag. (Everyone needs a home: Annual report 1998)

Notes on contributors

Sarah Banks is a senior lecturer in community and youth work at the University of Durham, UK. She teaches and researches in the field of professional ethics, community development and youth work, and has published several books on these themes.

Wilfred Diekmann is a lecturer in social educational care work at the Hogeschool van Amsterdam, the Netherlands. He teaches in the field of social work theory, methodology and ethics (especially youth care).

François Gillet is a lecturer in social education at the Pedagogical Department of the Haute Ecole de Bruxelles, Belgium. He teaches and researches in the field of psycho-pedagogics, practical training and professional ethics.

Henk Goovaerts is head of the Department of Social Work and senior lecturer at the KHLim in Belgium. He teaches professional ethics and political development in social work and has published several articles on these themes.

Helene Jacobson Pettersson is a lecturer and international coordinator in social work at the University of Kalmar, Sweden and postgraduate student in Social Work at the University of Växjö, Sweden. She teaches in the field of ethics and intercultural communication in social work.

Robert Langen is a lecturer at the Department of Social Work of the FHS Hochschule für Technik, Wirtschaft und Soziale Arbeit St. Gallen, Switzerland. He teaches in the field of social pedagogics and specialises in work with disabilities, behavioural problems and ethical themes emerging in this area.

Anne Liebing is a lecturer in social science at Roskilde Pædagogseminarium, Fröbel-højskolen in Denmark, which is part of CVU Øst, Denmark. She teaches in the field of social politics, social exclusion and inclusion and social pedagogics, especially aimed at professional work with children at risk and people with disabilities.

Birgitte Møller is a lecturer in social care work at Københavns Socialpædagogiske Seminarium, which is part of CVU Øst, Denmark. She teaches in the field of social pedagogics, professional care, youth work and the work with handicapped people and is specialised in management of social institutions in the pedagogical field.

Nils-Erik Nyboe is a teacher at Dannerseminariet, Northsealand, Denmark. He teaches pedagogics, social pedagogics and supervises in practical pedagogics and care. He is also the international coordinator of his school.

Kirsten Nøhr is a lecturer in social care work (Pedagogical Diploma-Study) at the CVU København & Nordsjælland, Denmark. She teaches in the field of social pedagogics, professional care, youth work and work with people with learning disabilities.

Frank Philippart is a senior lecturer in social work at the Hogeschool Brabant, The Netherlands. He teaches in the field of social work.

Françoise Ranson is responsible for vocational training (adults) in an Institute for Social Workers, I.R.F.F.E. Amiens, France. She teaches ethics in social work, accompaniment of people close to death or in bereavement.

Jochen Windheuser is a lecturer in psychology at the Katholische Fachhochschule Norddeutschland in Osnabrück, Germany. He teaches in social work education and contributes to projects with psychic ill patients, homeless people and multiproblem families.